Computer Forensics: Investigating Data and Image Files

EC-Council | Press

Book 3 of 4

C | HFI™

Computer | **Hacking Forensic**
INVESTIGATOR
Certification

CENGAGE
Learning·

Australia • Brazil • Mexico • Singapore • United Kingdom • United States

Computer Forensics: Investigating Data and Image Files (CHFI)

EC-Council | Press

SVP, GM Skills & Global Product Management: Dawn Gerrain

Product Director: Kathleen McMahon

Product Team Manager: Kristin McNary

Senior Director, Development: Marah Bellegarde

Product Development Manager: Leigh Hefferon

Managing Content Developer: Emma Newsom

Senior Content Developer: Natalie Pashoukos

Product Assistant: Abigail Pufpaff

Vice President, Marketing Services: Jennifer Ann Baker

Marketing Coordinator: Cassie Cloutier

Senior Production Director: Wendy Troeger

Production Director: Patty Stephan

Senior Content Project Manager: Brooke Greenhouse

Managing Art Director: Jack Pendleton

Software Development Manager: Pavan Ethakota

Cover Image(s):
Istockphoto.com/gong hangxu
Istockphoto.com/Turnervisual

EC-Council:

President | EC-Council: Jay Bavisi

Vice President, North America | EC-Council: Steven Graham

For product information and technology assistance, contact us at
Cengage Learning Customer & Sales Support, 1-800-354-9706

For permission to use material from this text or product, submit all requests online at **www.cengage.com/permissions**. Further permissions questions can be e-mailed to **permissionrequest@cengage.com**.

Library of Congress Control Number: 2016933691

ISBN: 978-1-305-88349-9

Cengage Learning
20 Channel Center Street
Boston, MA 02210
USA

Cengage Learning is a leading provider of customized learning solutions with employees residing in nearly 40 different countries and sales in more than 125 countries around the world. Find your local representative at **www.cengage.com**.

Cengage Learning products are represented in Canada by Nelson Education, Ltd.

To learn more about Cengage Learning, visit **www.cengage.com**.

Purchase any of our products at your local college store or at our preferred online store **www.cengagebrain.com**.

Printed in the United States of America
Print Number: 01   Print Year: 2016

Brief Table of Contents

Table of Contents

Preface

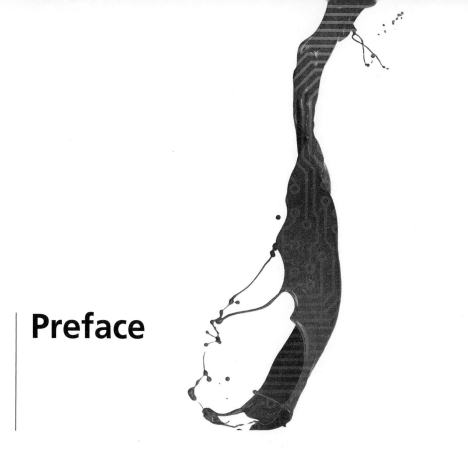

Hacking and electronic crimes sophistication is consistently growing at an exponential rate. Recent reports have indicated that cybercrime already surpasses the illegal drug trade! Unethical hackers, better known as *black hat hackers*, are preying on information systems of government, corporate, public, and private networks and are constantly testing the security mechanisms of these organizations to the limit with the sole aim of exploiting them and profiting from the exercise. High-profile crimes have proven that the traditional approach to computer security is simply not sufficient, even with the strongest perimeter; properly configured defense mechanisms such as firewalls, intrusion detection, and prevention systems; strong end-to-end encryption standards; and antivirus software. Hackers have proven their dedication and ability to systematically penetrate networks all over the world. In some cases, black hat hackers may be able to execute attacks so flawlessly that they can compromise a system, steal everything of value, and completely erase their tracks in less than 20 minutes!

The EC-Council | Press is dedicated to stopping hackers in their tracks.

About EC-Council

The International Council of Electronic Commerce Consultants, better known as EC-Council, was founded in late 2001 to address the need for well-educated and certified information security and e-business practitioners. EC-Council is a global, member-based organization comprised of industry and subject matter experts all working together to set the standards and raise the bar in information security certification and education.

EC-Council first developed the *Certified Ethical Hacker* (C|EH) program. The goal of this program is to teach the methodologies, tools, and techniques used by hackers. Leveraging the collective knowledge from hundreds of subject matter experts, the C|EH program has rapidly gained popularity around the globe and is now delivered in more than 120 countries by more than 600 authorized training centers. More than 120,000 information security practitioners have been trained.

C|EH is the benchmark for many government entities and major corporations around the world. Shortly after C|EH was launched, EC-Council developed the *Certified Security Analyst* (E|CSA). The goal of the E|CSA program is to teach groundbreaking analysis methods that must be applied while conducting advanced penetration testing. The E|CSA program leads to the *Licensed Penetration Tester* (L|PT) status. The *Computer Hacking Forensic Investigator* (C|HFI) was formed with the same design methodologies and has become a global standard in certification for computer forensics. EC-Council, through its impervious network of professionals and huge industry following, has developed various other programs in information security and e-business. EC-Council certifications are viewed as the essential certifications needed when standard configuration and security policy courses fall short. Being provided with a true, hands-on, tactical approach to security, individuals armed with the knowledge disseminated by EC-Council programs are securing networks around the world and beating the hackers at their own game.

About the EC-Council | Press

The EC-Council | Press was formed in late 2008 as a result of a cutting-edge partnership between global information security certification leader, EC-Council and leading global academic publisher, Cengage Learning. This partnership marks a revolution in academic textbooks and courses of study in information security, computer forensics, disaster recovery, and end-user security. By identifying the essential topics and content of EC-Council professional certification programs, and repurposing this world-class content to fit academic programs, the EC-Council | Press was formed. The academic community is now able to incorporate this powerful cutting-edge content into new and existing information security programs. By closing the gap between academic study and professional certification, students and instructors are able to leverage the power of rigorous academic focus and high-demand industry certification. The EC-Council | Press is set to revolutionize global information security programs and ultimately create a new breed of practitioners capable of combating the growing epidemic of cybercrime and the rising threat of cyber-war.

Computer Forensics Series

The EC-Council | Press *Computer Forensics* series, preparing learners for C|HFI certification, is intended for those studying to become police investigators and other law enforcement personnel, defense and military personnel, e-business security professionals, systems administrators, legal professionals, banking, insurance and other professionals, personnel within government agencies, and IT managers. The content of this program is designed to expose the learner to the process of detecting attacks and collecting evidence in a forensically sound manner with the intent to report crime and prevent future attacks. Advanced techniques in computer investigation and analysis with interest in generating potential legal evidence are included. In full, this series prepares the learner to identify evidence in computer-related crime and abuse cases as well as track the intrusive hacker's path through a client system.

Books in Series

- *Computer Forensics: Investigation Procedures and Response/9781305883475*
- *Computer Forensics: Investigating File and Operating Systems, Wireless Networks, and Storage/9781305883482*
- *Computer Forensics: Investigating Data and Image Files/9781305883499*
- *Computer Forensics: Investigating Network Intrusions and Cybercrime/9781305883505*

Investigating Data and Image Files

Investigating Data and Image Files provides a basic understanding of steganography, data acquisition and duplication, EnCase, how to recover deleted files and partitions, and image file forensics.

Chapter Contents

Chapter 1, *Steganography*, provides the history and classifications of steganography, explains the difference between steganography and cryptography as well as the essentials of stego-forensics and watermarking. Chapter 2, *Data Acquisition and Duplication*, focuses on how to determine the best data acquisition method, how to make sure crucial data is not lost, and the importance of data duplication. A description of the tools used for data acquisition and duplication is also included. Chapter 3, *Forensic Investigations Using EnCase*, includes coverage of this forensic software suite and how investigators can use EnCase to perform different forensic tasks. Chapter 4, *Recovering Deleted Files and Deleted Partitions*, covers deleting files and the recycling bin as well as file recovery and deleting and recovering partitions. Chapter 5, *Image File Forensics*, covers the various methods that can be used to recover graphics files. It also highlights the various image recovery, steganalysis, and viewing tools that are used and the salient features of these tools.

Chapter Features

Many features are included in each chapter and all are designed to enhance the reader's learning experience. Features include:

- *Objectives* begin each chapter and focus the learner on the most important concepts in the chapter.
- *What If?*, found in each chapter, presents short scenarios followed by questions that challenge the learner to arrive at an answer or solution to the problem presented.
- *Chapter Summary*, at the end of each chapter, serves as a review of the key concepts covered in the chapter.

- *Key Terms* are designed to familiarize the learner with terms that will be used within the chapter.

- *Review Questions* allow learners to test their comprehension of the chapter content.

- *Hands-On Projects* encourage learners to apply the knowledge they have gained after finishing the chapter. Files for the Hands-On Projects can be found in the MindTap or on the Student Resource Center. Visit *www.cengagebrain.com* for a link to the Student Resource Center.

MindTap

MindTap for Computer Forensics Series (CHFI) is an online learning solution designed to help students master the skills they need in today's workforce. Research shows employers need critical thinkers, troubleshooters, and creative problem solvers to stay relevant in our fast-paced, technology-driven world. MindTap helps users achieve this with assignments and activities that provide hands-on practice, real-life relevance, and mastery of difficult concepts. Students are guided through assignments that progress from basic knowledge and understanding to more challenging problems.

All MindTap activities and assignments are tied to learning objectives. The hands-on exercises provide real-life application and practice. Readings and "Whiteboard Shorts" support the lecture, while "In the News" assignments encourage students to stay current. Pre- and post-course assessments allow you to measure how much students have learned using analytics and reporting that makes it easy to see where the class stands in terms of progress, engagement, and completion rates. Use the content and learning path as is, or pick and choose how the material will wrap around your own. You control what the students see and when they see it. Learn more at *www.cengage.com/mindtap/*.

Student Resource Center

The Student Resource Center contains all the files you need to complete the Hands-On Projects found at the end of the chapters. Visit *www.cengagebrain.com* to access the Student Resource Center.

Additional Instructor Resources

Free to all instructors who adopt the *Investigation Procedures and Response* book for their courses is a complete package of instructor resources. These resources are available from the Cengage Learning Web site, *www.cengagebrain.com*, by going to the product page for this book in the online catalog and choosing "Instructor Downloads."

Resources include:

- *Instructor's Manual*: This manual includes course objectives and additional information to help your instruction.

- *Cengage Learning Testing Powered by Cognero*: A flexible, online system that allows you to import, edit, and manipulate content from the text's test bank or elsewhere, including your own favorite test questions; create multiple test versions in an instant; and deliver tests from your LMS, your classroom, or wherever you want.

- *PowerPoint Presentations*: A set of Microsoft PowerPoint slides is included for each chapter. These slides are meant to be used as teaching aids for classroom presentations, to be made available to students for chapter reviews, or to be printed for classroom distribution. Instructors are also at liberty to add their own slides.

- *Labs*: These are additional hands-on activities to provide more practice for your students.

- *Assessment Activities*: These are additional assessment opportunities including discussion questions, writing assignments, Internet research activities, and homework assignments along with a final cumulative project.

- *Final Exam*: This exam provides a comprehensive assessment of *Investigation Procedures and Response* content.

Cengage Learning Tech Connection: Information Security Community

This site was created for learners and instructors to find out about the latest in information security news and technology.

Visit *http://community.cengage.com/InfoSec2/* to:

- Learn what's new in information security through live news feeds, videos, and podcasts;

- Connect with your peers and security experts through blogs and forums;

- Browse our online catalog.

How to Become C|HFI Certified

Today's battles between corporations, governments, and countries are no longer fought only in the typical arenas of boardrooms or battlefields using physical force. Now the battlefield starts in the technical realm, which ties into most facets of modern day life. The C|HFI certification focuses on the necessary skills to identify an intruder's footprints and to properly gather the necessary evidence to prosecute. The C|HFI certification is primarily targeted at police and other law enforcement personnel, defense and military personnel, e-business security professionals, systems administrators, legal professionals, banking, insurance and other professionals, personnel in government agencies, and IT managers. This certification will ensure that you have the knowledge and skills to identify, track, and prosecute the cybercriminal.

C|HFI certification exams are available through the EC-Council Exam Portal. To finalize your certification after your training, you must take the certification exam through an EC-Council Testing Center (ETC). To take the certification exam, follow these steps:

1. Inquire about purchasing an exam voucher by visiting the EC-Council community site: *http://ace.eccouncil.org*, if one was not purchased with your book.

   Once you have your exam voucher, visit *https://cert.eccouncil.org/doc/PROCTORU&EC CEXAMGUIDE.pdf*.

2. Schedule your exam, using the information on your voucher.

3. Take and pass the C|HFI certification examination with a score of 70 percent or better.

Additional EC-Council | Press Products

Ethical Hacking and Countermeasures Series

The EC-Council | Press *Ethical Hacking and Countermeasures* series is intended for those studying to become security officers, auditors, security professionals, site administrators, and anyone who is concerned about or responsible for the integrity of the network infrastructure. The series includes a broad base of topics in offensive network security, ethical hacking, as well as network defense and countermeasures. The content of this series is designed to immerse learners into an interactive environment where they will be shown how to scan, test, hack, and secure information systems. A wide variety of tools, viruses, and malware is presented in these books, providing a complete understanding of the tactics and tools used by hackers. By gaining a thorough understanding of how hackers operate, ethical hackers are able to set up strong countermeasures and defensive systems to protect their organization's critical infrastructure and information. The series, when used in its entirety, helps prepare readers to take and succeed on the C|EH certification exam from EC-Council.

Books in Series

- *Ethical Hacking and Countermeasures: Attack Phases*/9781305883437
- *Ethical Hacking and Countermeasures: Threats and Defense Mechanisms*/9781305883444
- *Ethical Hacking and Countermeasures: Web Applications and Data Servers*/9781305883451
- *Ethical Hacking and Countermeasures: Secure Network Operating Systems and Infrastructures*/9781305883468

EC-Council's Supporting Events

TakeDownCon

TakeDownCon is a highly technical forum that focuses on the latest vulnerabilities, the most potent exploits, and current security threats. The best and the brightest come to share their knowledge, giving delegates the opportunity to learn about the industry's most important issue. With two days and two dynamic tracks, delegates will spend Day 1 on the Attack, learning how even the most protected systems can be breached. Day 2 is dedicated to Defense, and delegates will learn if their defense mechanisms are on par to thwart nefarious and persistent attacks.

For more information, visit the Web site: *www.takedowncon.com*.

Hacker Halted

Hacker Halted builds on the educational foundation of EC-Council's courses in ethical hacking, computer forensics, pen testing, and many others. Hacker Halted brings the industry's leading researchers, practitioners, ethical hackers, and other top IT security professionals together to discuss current issues facing our industry. Hacker Halted has been delivered globally in countries such as Egypt, Mexico, Malaysia, Hong Kong, Iceland, and in the United States, in cities such as Myrtle Beach, Miami, and most recently in Atlanta.

For more information, visit the Web site: *www.hackerhalted.com*.

Global CyberLympics

Global CyberLympics is an online ethical hacking computer network defense competition. The goal is to raise awareness of increased education and ethics in information security through a series of cyber competitions that encompass forensics, ethical hacking, and defense. Teams are made up of four to six players, and each round serves as an elimination round until the top teams remain. The top teams from each region get invited to play live in-person at the world finals.

For more information, visit the Web site: *www.cyberlympics.org.*

Acknowledgments

Michael H. Goldner is recently retired as Dean of EC-Council University. He has been involved in the information security arena for over 20 years and has dedicated the last 15 years to developing hands-on academic curricula to help train the world's future cyber leaders. He received his Juris Doctorate from Stetson University College of Law and his undergraduate degree from Miami University. He is an active member of the American Bar Association and a member of the Cyber Law subcommittee. He is a member of IEEE, ISSA ISC2, ISACA, and PMI and holds a number of industrially recognized certifications, including C|CISO, CISSP, CISM, CEI, CEH, CHFI, MCT, MCSE/Security, MCSA, Security+, Network+, and A+.

Michael has worked closely with EC-Council and Cengage Learning in the creation of this EC-Council Press series on information security and computer forensics, and is passionate about creating a viable international leadership corps to guide our electronically connected society into a safe and prosperous future.

Angela Herring authored the hands-on projects at the end of each chapter. Herring is the Director of Distance Learning at Wilson Community College where her primary job function includes administration of the learning management system and faculty training. Herring plays an integral role in several campus-wide initiatives including Accessibility, Online Tutoring, and Student Success. Previously, she served as instructor and advisor of the Information Systems Security program for 10 years where she taught courses in security awareness, ethical hacking, and web development. Her educational background includes a B.S. in Business Administration/Computer Information Systems, a M.A.Ed. in Instructional Technology, and a Graduate Certificate in Information Assurance.

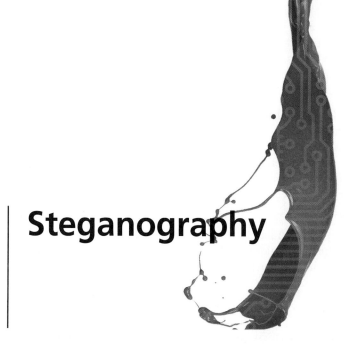

chapter 1

Steganography

After completing this chapter, you should be able to:

- Understand steganography
- Recount the history of steganography
- Explain the classifications of steganography
- Identify image steganography
- Detect steganography
- Explain the differences between steganography and cryptography
- Explain stego-forensics
- Explain watermarking
- Select appropriate steganography tools

What If?

Jeremy Johnson, 26, was hired by Adams Central School District as a teacher. During his tenure as a teacher, there were rumors around the school campus about an inappropriate relationship between him and a female student. Both denied the rumors. Since school officials had no evidence of the relationship, they could only issue a warning. Several months later, the student told her cousins about the relationship. This triggered an investigation by the Adams County Sheriff's Department.

The police searched Johnson's home. Johnson's bedroom matched the description given by the student in an interview with a female police officer. Johnson continued to deny the girl's claims concerning their sexual relationship. During the search, they seized his laptop and desktop computer. The investigators were able to verify that Johnson and the student exchanged e-mails. Johnson had reportedly set up an e-mail account for the girl in his wife's name. Though the e-mails were not explicit, the investigators could prove that Johnson and the student had been having a sexual relationship.

Later, the forensic examiner found that Johnson had been trading child pornography over the Internet. He had hundreds of nude pictures of children obviously under the age of 18. He had tried to hide the images by putting them in a folder labeled "music."

Jeremy Johnson was arrested and jailed on 19 charges of child seduction, a Class D felony.

- How could Johnson have used steganography to hide his crime?
- What tools could law enforcement have used to uncover the use of steganography?

Introduction to Steganography

Steganography is the practice of embedding hidden messages within a carrier medium. Mathematicians, military personnel, and scientists have used it for centuries. The use of steganography dates back to ancient Egypt. Today steganography, in its digital form, is widely used on the Internet and in a variety of multimedia forms.

Modern steganography works by replacing bits of useless or unused data in regular computer files with bits of different, invisible information. When a file cannot be encrypted, the next best option for safe transfer is steganography. Steganography can also be used to supplement encryption. When used in this manner, steganography provides a double measure of protection, as the encrypted file, once deciphered, will not allow a message hidden by steganography to be seen. The receiver of the file has to use special software to decipher a message hidden by steganography.

Stegosystem Model

A **stegosystem** is the mechanism that is used in performing steganography (Figure 1-1). The following components make up a stegosystem:

- *Embedded message*: The original secret message to be hidden behind the cover medium
- *Cover medium*: The medium used to hide the message

- *Stego-key*: The secret key used to encrypt and decrypt the message
- *Stego-medium*: The combined cover medium and embedded message

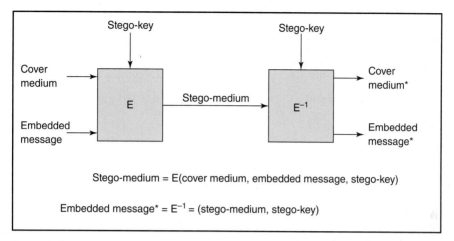

Figure 1-1   A stegosystem is the mechanism used to embed a hidden message within a cover medium.

Application of Steganography

Steganography can be used for a variety of legal and illegal uses. It can be used for the following purposes:

- *Medical records*: Steganography is used in medical records to avoid any mix-up of patients' records. Every patient has an EPR (electronic patient record), which has examinations and other medical records stored in it.

- *Workplace communication*: Steganography can be used as an effective method for employees who desire privacy in the workplace to bypass the normal communication channels. In this area, steganography can be an obstacle to network security.

- *Digital music*: Steganography is also used to protect music from being copied by introducing subtle changes into a music file that act as a digital signature. BlueSpike Technology removes a few select tones in a narrow band. Verance adds signals that are out of the frequency range detectable by the human ear. Others adjust the sound by changing the frequency slightly. Digital audio files can also be modified to carry a large amount of information. Some files simply indicate that the content is under copyright. More sophisticated steganography versions can include information about the artist.

- *Terrorism*: Certain extremist Web sites have been known to use pictures and text to secretly communicate messages to terrorist cells operating globally. Servers and computers globally provide a new twist on this covert activity.

- *The movie industry*: Steganography can also be used as copyright protection for DVDs and VCDs. The DVD copy-protection program is designed to support a copy generation management system. Second-generation DVD players with digital video recording capabilities continue to be introduced in the black market. To protect itself against piracy, the movie industry needs to copyright DVDs.

Classification of Steganography

Steganography is classified into the following three major categories (Figure 1-2):

- Technical steganography
- Linguistic steganography
- Digital steganography

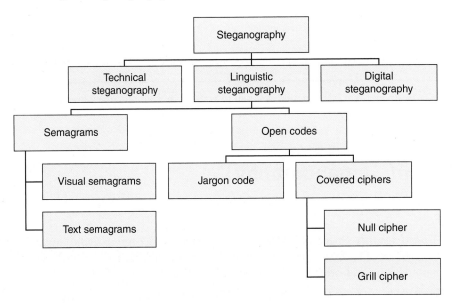

Figure 1-2 Steganography is classified into three main categories.

Technical Steganography

In technical steganography, physical or chemical methods are used to hide the existence of a message. Technical steganography can include the following methods:

- *Invisible inks*: These are colorless liquids that need heating and lighting in order to be read. For example, if onion juice and milk are used to write a message, the writing cannot be seen unless heat is applied, which makes the ink turn brown.
- *Microdots*: This method shrinks a page-sized photograph to 1 mm in diameter. The photograph is reduced with the help of a reverse microscope.

Linguistic Steganography

Linguistic steganography hides messages in the carrier in several ways. The two main techniques of linguistic steganography involve the use of semagrams and open codes.

Semagrams Semagrams hide information through the use of signs or symbols. Objects or symbols can be embedded in data to send messages. Semagrams can be classified into the following types:

- *Visual semagrams*: In this technique a drawing, painting, letter, music, or any other symbol is used to hide the information. For example, the position of items on a desk or Web site may be used to hide some kind of message.

- *Text semagrams*: In this technique, a message is hidden by changing the appearance of the carrier text. Text can be changed by modifying the font size, using extra spaces between words, or by using different flourishes in letters or handwritten text.

Open Codes Open codes make use of openly readable text. This text contains words or sentences that can be hidden in a reversed or vertical order. The letters should be in selected locations of the text. Open codes can be either jargon codes or covered ciphers.

- *Jargon codes*: In this type of open code, a certain language is used that can only be understood by a particular group of people while remaining meaningless to others. A jargon message is similar to a substitution cipher in many respects, but rather than replacing individual letters the words themselves are changed.

- *Covered ciphers*: This technique hides the message in a carrier medium that is visible to everyone. Any person who knows how the message is hidden can extract this type of message. Covered ciphers can be both null and grill ciphers.

  - *Null ciphers*: Null ciphers hide the message within a large amount of useless data. The original data may be mixed with the unused data in any order—for example, diagonally, vertically, or in reverse order—allowing only the person who knows the order to understand it.

  - *Grill ciphers*: It is possible to encrypt plaintext by writing it onto a sheet of paper through a separate pierced sheet of paper or cardboard. When an identical pierced sheet is placed on the message, the original text can be read. The grill system is difficult to crack and decipher, as only the person with the grill (sheet of paper) can decipher the hidden message.

Digital Steganography

In digital steganography, the secret messages are hidden in a digital medium. The following techniques are used in digital steganography:

- Injection
- Least significant bit (LSB)
- Transform-domain techniques
- Spread-spectrum encoding
- Perceptual masking
- File generation
- Statistical method
- Distortion technique

Injection With the injection technique, the secret information is placed inside a carrier or host file. The secret message is directly inserted into a host medium, which could be a picture, sound file, or video clip. The drawback to this technique is that the size of the host file increases, making it easy to detect. This can be overcome by deleting the original file once the file with the secret message is created. It is difficult to detect the presence of any secret message once the original file is deleted.

Least Significant Bit (LSB) With the **least-significant-bit** (LSB) technique, the rightmost bit in the binary notation is substituted with a bit from the embedded message. The rightmost bit has the least impact on the binary data. If an attacker knows that this technique is used, then the data are vulnerable.

Figure 1-3 shows a basic LSB approach. Bit planes of a grayscale image are imprinted with the most significant bit (MSB) on top. The dark boxes represent binary value 0, and the light boxes represent binary value 1. The LSB plane of the cover image is replaced with the hidden data.

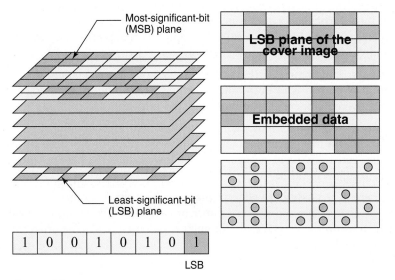

Figure 1-3 LSB substitutes the rightmost bit in the binary notation with a bit from the embedded message.

Transform-Domain Techniques A transformed space is generated when a file is compressed at the time of transmission. This transformed space is used to hide data. The three transform techniques used when embedding a message are: discrete cosine transform (DCT), discrete Fourier transform (DFT), and discrete wavelet transform (DWT). These techniques embed the secret data in the cover at the time of the transmission process. The transformation can be applied either to an entire carrier file or to its subparts. The embedding process is performed by modifying the coefficients, which are selected based on the protection required. The hidden data in the transform domain is present in more robust areas, and it is highly resistant to signal processing.

Example: Images sent through Internet channels typically use JPEG format because it compresses itself when the file is closed. A JPEG file makes an approximation of itself to reduce the file's size and removes the excess bits from the image. This change and approximation results in transform space that can be used to hide information.

Spread-Spectrum Encoding Spread-spectrum encoding encodes a small-band signal into a wide-band cover. The encoder modulates a small-band signal over a carrier.

Spread-spectrum encoding can be used in the following ways:

- *Direct sequence*: In direct-sequence encoding, the information is divided into small parts that are allocated to the frequency channel of the spectrum. The data signal is combined during transmission with a higher data-rate bit sequence that divides the data based on the predetermined spread ratio. The redundant nature of the data-rate bit sequence code is useful to the signal-resist interference, allowing the original data to be recovered.

- *Frequency hopping*: This technique is used to divide the bandwidth's spectrum into many possible broadcast frequencies. Frequency hopping devices require less power and are cheaper, but are less reliable when compared to direct sequence spectrum systems.

Perceptual Masking Perceptual masking is the interference of one perceptual stimulus with another, resulting in a decrease in perceptual effectiveness. This type of steganography makes one signal hard to identify due to the presence of another signal.

File Generation Rather than selecting a cover to hide a message, this technique generates a new cover file solely for the purpose of hiding data. A picture is created that has a hidden message in it. In the modern form of file generation, a spam-mimic program is used. Spam mimic embeds the secret message into a spam message that can be e-mailed to any destination.

Statistical Method This method uses a one-bit steganographic scheme. It embeds one bit of information in a digital carrier, creating a statistical change. A statistical change in the cover is indicated as a 1. A 0 indicates that a bit was left unchanged (Figure 1-4). The work is based on the receiver's ability to differentiate between modified and unmodified covers.

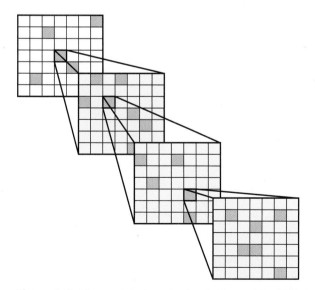

Figure 1-4   The statistical method embeds one bit of information in a digital carrier.

Distortion Technique This technique creates a change in the cover object in order to hide the information. An encoder performs a sequence of modifications to the cover that corresponds to a secret message. The secret message is recovered by comparing the distorted cover with the original. The decoder in this technique needs access to the original cover file.

Digital File Types

The various techniques used in steganography are applied differently depending on the type of file that is being used to encode the message. The four digital file types are text, image, audio, and video files.

Text Files

The following steganography methods are used in text files:

- Open-space
- Syntactic
- Semantic

Open-Space Steganography This method uses white space on the printed page. Open-space methods can be categorized in the following three ways:

- *Intersentence spacing*: This method encodes a binary message by inserting one or two spaces after every terminating character. This method is inefficient since it requires more space for a small message, and the white spaces can be easily spotted.
- *End-of-line spacing*: Secret data is placed at the end of a line in the form of spaces. This allows more room to insert a message but can create problems when the program automatically removes extra spaces or the document is printed as hard copy.
- *Interword spacing*: This method uses right justification, by which the justification spaces can be adjusted to allow binary encoding. A single space between words is 0, and two spaces is 1.

Syntactic Steganography This method manipulates punctuation to hide messages.

Look at the following example:

- Laptop, iPod, USB
- Laptop iPod USB

The punctuation marks are missing in the second phrase. These punctuation marks can be used to hide the message.

Semantic Steganography This method of data hiding involves changing the words themselves. Semantic steganography assigns two synonyms primary and secondary values. When decoded, the primary value is read as 1 and the secondary as 0.

Image Files

Image files commonly use the following formats:

- *Graphics Interchange Format (GIF)*: GIF files are compressed image files that make use of a compression algorithm developed by CompuServe. GIF files are based on a palette of 256 colors. They are mainly used for small icons and animated images since they do not have the color ranges needed for high-quality photos.

- *Joint Photographic Experts Group (JPEG)*: JPEG files are the proper format for photo images that need to be small in size. JPEG files are compressed by 90%, or to one-tenth, of the size of the data.

- *Tagged Image File Format (TIFF)*: The TIFF file format was designed to minimize the problems with mixed file formats. This file format did not evolve from a de facto standard. It was made as the standard image file format for image file exchange.

The following steganography techniques are used to hide a message in an image file:

- LSB insertion

- Masking and filtering

- Algorithms and transformation

LSB Insertion Using the LSB insertion method, the binary representation of the hidden data can be used to overwrite the LSB of each byte inside the image. If the image properties indicate that the image is 24-bit color, the net change is minimal and can be indiscernible to the human eye.

The following steps are involved in hiding the data:

- The steganography tool makes a copy of an image palette with the help of the red, green, and blue (RGB) model.

- Each pixel of the eight-bit binary number LSB is substituted with one bit of the hidden message.

- A new RGB color in the copied palette is produced.

- With the new RGB color, the pixel is changed to an eight-bit binary number.

Look at the following example:

```
01001101 00101110 10101110 10001010
10101111 10100010 00101011 10101011
```

Seen above are the adjacent pixels made up of eight bits. If the letter *H* is represented by binary digits, 01001000 needs to be hidden in this file, and the data would need to be compressed before being hidden.

After *H* is combined, the changed binary values would be as seen below:

```
01001100 00101111 10101110 10001010
10101111 10100010 00101010 10101010
```

Eight bits, which is four of the LSBs, have been successfully hidden. The above example is meant to be a high-level overview. This method can be applied to eight-bit color images.

Grayscale images are also used for steganographic purposes. The drawback to these methods is that they can be detected by anyone who knows where to search for them.

Masking and Filtering Masking and filtering techniques are commonly used on 24-bit and grayscale images. Grayscale images that hide information are similar to watermarks on paper and are sometimes used as digital versions. Masking images entails changing the luminescence of the masked area. The smaller the luminescent change, the less chance there is that it can be detected. Steganography images that are masked keep a higher fidelity rate than LSB through compression, cropping, and image processing. The reason that images encoded with masking have less degradation under JPEG compression is because the message is hidden in significant areas of the picture. The tool named Jpeg-Jsteg takes advantage of the compression of JPEG and keeps high message fidelity. This program uses a message and lossless cover image as input and produces an output image in JPEG format.

Algorithms and Transformation Mathematical functions can be used to hide data that are in compression algorithms. In this technique, the data are embedded in the cover image by changing the coefficients of an image (e.g. discrete cosine transform coefficients).

If information is embedded in the spatial domain, it may be subjected to loss if the image undergoes any processing techniques like compression. To overcome this problem, the image would need to be embedded with information that can be hidden in the frequency domain, as the digital data is not continuous enough to analyze the data of the image that transformations are applied on.

Audio Files

Hiding information in an audio file can be done by using either LSB or frequencies that are inaudible to the human ear. Frequencies over 20,000 Hz cannot be detected by the human ear.

Information can also be hidden using musical tones with a substitution scheme. For example, tone F could represent 0, and tone C could represent 1. By using the substitution technique a simple musical piece can be composed with a secret message, or an existing piece can be used with an encoded scheme that represents a message.

Low-Bit Encoding in Audio Files Digital steganography is based on the fact that artifacts, such as bitmaps and audio files, contain redundant information. Compression techniques such as JPEG and MP3 remove parts of the redundancy, allowing the files to be compressed. By using the DigSteg tool, the computer forensic investigator can replace some of the redundant information with other data.

Low-bit encoding replaces the LSB of information in each sampling point with a coded binary string. The low-bit method encodes large amounts of hidden data into an audio signal at the expense of producing significant noise in the upper frequency range.

Phase Coding Phase coding involves substituting an initial audio segment with a reference phase that represents the data. This method is carried out using the following steps:

1. The original sound sequence is shortened into segments.
2. Each segment creates a matrix of the phase and magnitude by using the DFT algorithm.

3. The phase difference is calculated between each adjacent segment.

4. New phase frames are created for all other segments.

5. A new segment is created by combining the new phase and the original magnitude.

6. These new segments are combined together to create the encoded output.

Spread Spectrum In most communication channels, audio data is limited to a narrow range of frequencies to protect the bandwidth of the channel. Unlike phase coding, direct-sequence spread spectrum (DSSS) introduces some random noise to the signal. The encoded data is spread across as much of the frequency spectrum as possible.

Spread spectrum is used in audio files both to embed data in the audio file and to send the audio file.

Echo Data Hiding In this technique, an echo is introduced into the original signal. Three properties of this echo can then be varied to hide data:

- Initial amplitude
- Decay rate
- Offset

Video Files

Discrete cosine transform (DCT) manipulation is used to add secret data at the time of the transformation process of the video. The techniques used in audio and image files can also be used in video files, as video consists of audio and images. A large number of secret messages can be hidden in video files because a video is a moving stream of images and sound. Due to this, an individual watching the video will not observe any distortion in the video caused by the hiding of data.

Steganographic File System

A steganographic file system is a method used to store files that encrypts and hides the data within those files. It hides the user's data in other, seemingly random files, allowing users to give names and passwords for some files while keeping others secret.

A steganographic file system is used to overcome the drawback of using individual files for data hiding. The following methods are used to construct a steganographic file system:

- Method 1:
  - Program operates using a set of cover files with initially random content.
  - The cover files are modified to store data files.
  - Cover files should be large enough to ensure that all attempts to access cover files remain computationally infeasible.

- Method 2:
  - ○ File system begins with random data.
  - ○ The encrypted blocks are written to the pseudorandom locations using the key acquired from the filename and directory password to hide the file blocks in random data. When the file system continues to be written to, collisions occur and the blocks are overwritten, allowing only a small portion of the disk space to be safely utilized.
  - ○ Multiple copies of each block should be written.
  - ○ A method to identify the blocks when they are overwritten is also required.

Cryptography

Cryptography is the art of writing text or data in a secret code. It involves encrypting plaintext data into an unreadable format called a ciphertext. This encryption process is based on mathematical algorithms. These algorithms use a secret key for secure encryption (Figure 1-5).

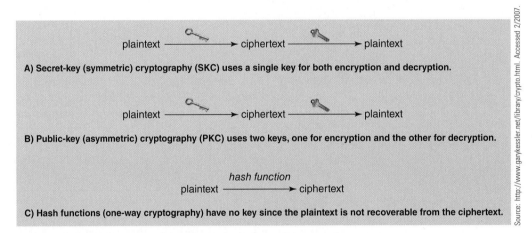

Figure 1-5   Cryptography can be performed in three different ways.

The following are three types of cryptographic schemes used:

- Secret-key (or symmetric) cryptography
- Public-key (or asymmetric) cryptography
- Hash function

In each of these schemes the primary unencrypted data is plaintext, which is encrypted into ciphertext.

Model of a Cryptosystem

A cryptosystem is a pair of algorithms that use a key to convert plaintext to ciphertext and back again. Figure 1-6 illustrates the cryptography process. The following key explains the symbols:

- Plaintext M: The original text to be encrypted to form the ciphertext
- k_e: The key used for encrypting the message
- Ciphertext C: The text obtained after encrypting the original message: Ciphertext $C = Ek_e(M)$
- k_d: The key used for decrypting the ciphertext: Plaintext $M = Dk_d(C)$, where $C = Ek_e(M)$

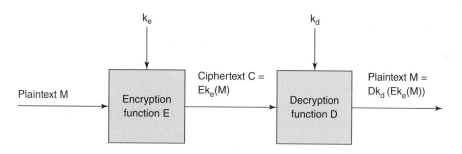

Figure 1-6   A cryptosystem uses a key to convert plaintext to ciphertext.

Steganography Versus Cryptography

Steganography is defined as the art of hiding data within other data. It replaces bits of unused data from various media files with other bits that, when assembled, reveal a hidden message. The hidden data can be plaintext, ciphertext, an audio clip, or an image.

In cryptography an encrypted message that is communicated can be detected but cannot be read. In steganography, the existence of the message is hidden. Steganography is used to hide information when encryption is not a safe option. From a security point of view, steganography should be used to hide a file in an encrypted format. This is done to ensure that even if the encrypted file is decrypted, the message will still remain hidden.

Another contrast between steganography and cryptography is that the former requires caution when reusing pictures or sound files, while the latter requires caution when reusing keys.

In steganography, only one key is used to hide and extract data. In cryptography, the same key or two different keys for encryption and decryption can be used.

Public Key Infrastructure

Public key infrastructure (PKI) is used for secure and private data exchange over the Internet. It uses a public and private cryptographic key pair that is obtained and given to the public key owner. PKI provides a digital certificate that can identify an individual or organization and directory services that can store and, when necessary, revoke the certificates. It uses

PKC, which is the most commonly used method on the Internet for authenticating a message sender or encrypting a message.

PKI consists of the following components:

- A certificate authority (CA) that issues and verifies the digital certificate
- A registration authority (RA) that acts as the verifier for the certificate authority before a digital certificate is issued to a request
- One or more directories where the certificates (with their public keys) are held
- Key management protocols

The primary goal of a key management scheme is to provide two communicating devices with a common or shared cryptographic key. The term *session key* is used to identify a short-lived key. This key does not require a session-based communication model. *Master key* is used to denote a key having a longer life period than a session key.

Watermarking

Traditionally, paper was manufactured from wet fiber, which was then subjected to high pressure to extract any moisture present in it. If the press mold had a pattern in it, that pattern, or watermark, would be left on the paper. This term has been incorporated into the term *digital watermark* in the technology field, but the meaning is essentially the same. **Digital watermarks** are, in essence, digital stamps embedded into digital signals. A digital stamp can contain many kinds of data, and can be both visible and invisible. Often, the digital data found hidden in a watermark are a digital multimedia object. While digital images are most often mentioned in reference to digital watermarking, it is important to remember that watermarks can be applied to other forms of digital data such as audio and video segments.

Application of Watermarking

Watermarking is used to facilitate the following processes:

- Embedding copyright statements into images that provide authentication to the owner of the data
- Monitoring and tracking copyright material automatically on the Web
- Providing automatic audits of radio transmissions. These audits show any music or advertisement that is broadcasted
- Supporting data augmentation. This enables users to add more information to the existing data present on the Web
- Supporting fingerprint applications

Steganography Versus Watermarking

The main purpose of steganography is to hide a message m in data d to form new data D, which is different from d, so that a third person cannot detect the m in D. Conversely, the main purpose of watermarking is to hide the data *m* in data *d* to form new data *D* so that a third person cannot remove or replace the *m* in *D*. Steganography hides the message in one-to-one communication, while watermarking hides the message in one-to-many communication. The main goal of steganography is to protect the data from detection, while that of watermarking is to protect data from distortion by others.

In steganography a message of any length can be hidden, whereas in watermarking only small messages can be hidden. Steganography is used for the purpose of secret communication, while watermarking is used for authentication and copyright protection.

Categories of Watermarks

Watermarks are split into two categories: visible and invisible.

- *Visible*: A visible watermark is the most robust as it is not part of the foundation of the image. The watermark's presence is clearly noticeable and often difficult to remove. A good example of a visible watermark is a television identification logo that appears on a television screen. The watermark can be either solid or semitransparent. Removing it would require a great deal of work.

- *Invisible*: The main purpose of an invisible watermark is to identify and verify a particular piece of information in data. An invisible watermark is imperceptible but can be extracted through computational methods. An invisible watermark contains information about the watermark itself or the information present in the image that is hiding the data. The data hidden in the image can be accessed with a password, called a watermark key. There is a big difference between a watermark key and an encryption key. A watermark key is used only for watermarks, whereas an encryption key is used for information that is to be encrypted.

Watermarks and Compression

The application of watermarks in the modern world mainly concerns images, audio, and video. Watermarks are used in the case of MP3s and DVDs as a tool to ensure copyrights are enforced.

Types of Watermarks

- *Semifragile*: Semifragile watermarks are used at the time of soft-image authentication and integrity verifications. They are robust to any common image processing of loose compression, but are fragile in case of any malicious tampering that changes the image content.

- *Fragile*: Fragile watermarks are less robust when modified. A small change in the content will destroy the embedded information and show that an attack has occurred. Any tampering with the image will modify its integrity.

- *Robust*: A robust watermark can be either visible or invisible. Robust watermarks are resistant to any kind of attack and will not affect the quality of the data. They are difficult to remove or damage. Robust watermarks are used in the case of copyright protection and access control. Most of these are found on television broadcasts during which the channels impose their logos in the corner of the screen to let people know what they are viewing and to signify copyright.

Digimarc's Digital Watermarking

Digimarc's digital watermarking technique enables users to embed a digital code into an image, audio, video, or text file. This digital code is unnoticeable in normal use and can be detected only by computers and software.

Digimarc's digital watermarking is used to embed copyright messages into the image, video, and audio files that provide authentication to the owner of the data.

The image gets split into a number of subimages. A Web browser puts all the pieces of the images together at display time, making a new image that is an exact replica of the original image. Both images are watermarked with Digimarcs, but the watermark is not readable in a small, partitioned image. Because all marking techniques need a marked image of minimal size, it is difficult to detect the mark from the image. It works because it is hard for copyright marking techniques to embed the watermark in an image having a size of less than 100 × 100 pixels. In addition, the bandwidth required for the embedding process is less.

Attacks on Watermarking

Robustness Attack This attack attempts to remove watermarks from an image. It can be divided into the following categories:

- *Signal-processing attacks*: These attacks apply techniques such as compression, filtering, resizing, printing, and scanning to remove the watermark.

- *Analytical and algorithmic attacks*: These attacks use algorithmic techniques of watermark insertion and detection to remove the watermark from the image.

- *Presentation attacks*: Presentation attacks are carried out to change the watermarked data in such a way that a detector cannot detect it. The watermark will appear as it did before the attack. It is not necessary to eliminate the watermark to carry out the attack. The following instances are examples of presentation attacks:

  ◦ An automated detector cannot detect the misalignment of a watermarked image.

  ◦ A detector cannot detect the rotation and enlargement of a watermark.

- *Interpretation attacks*: Interpretation attacks catch the weakness of watermarks, such as wrong and multiple interpretations. A watermark can be created from the existing watermark image with the same strength as the original watermark.

- *Legal attacks*: Legal attacks mainly target digital information and copyright laws. Attackers can change the watermarked copyrights in order to create doubts about copyright in a court of law. These attacks depend upon the following conditions:

  ◦ Existing and future legislation on copyright laws and digital information ownership

  ◦ The credibility of the owner and the attacker

  ◦ The financial strength of the owner and the attacker

  ◦ The expert witnesses

  ◦ The competence of the lawyers

The following techniques are commonly used to remove watermarks:

- *Collusion attack*: A collusion attack is carried out by searching for a number of different objects having the same watermark, allowing the forensic investigator to isolate and remove the watermark by comparing the copies.

- *Jitter attack*: A jitter attack upsets the placement of the bits that identify a watermark by applying a jitter effect to the image. By applying a jitter effect, the forensic investigator is able to gauge the integrity of the watermark.

- *StirMark*: A StirMark attack can be applied to small distortions that are designed to simulate the printing or scanning process. If a hard-copy photograph has been scanned, it would appear obvious that subtle distortions are introduced, no matter how careful the user is. The StirMark attack can be used for JPEG scaling and rotation. This attack is effective, as some watermarks are resistant to only one type of modification.

- *Anti–soft bot*: A benefit of watermarking in the realm of the Internet is the ability to use software robots, sometimes called soft bots or spiders, to search through Web pages for watermarked images. If the soft bot finds a watermarked image, it can use the information to determine if there is a copyright violation.

- *Attacks on echo hiding*: Echo hiding is a signal processing technique that places information into an audio data stream in the form of closely spaced echoes. These echoes place digital tags into the sound file with minimal sound degradation. Echo hiding is also resistant to jitter attacks, making a removal attack the usual method for getting rid of the watermark. In echo hiding, most echo delays are between 0.5 and 3 milliseconds; in anything above 3 milliseconds the echo becomes noticeable.

Mosaic Attack

A mosaic attack works by splitting an image into multiple pieces and stitching them back together using JavaScript code. In this attack the marked image can be unmarked, and later all the pixels are rendered in a similar fashion to the original marked image.

This attack was prompted by automatic copyright detection systems that contain watermarking techniques and crawlers that download images from the Internet to determine whether or not they are watermarked.

Mosaic Attack—JavaScript Code

```
<nobr>
<img SRC="kings_chapel_wmk1.jpg' BORDER="0' ALT="1/6' width="116'
height="140">
<img SRC="kings_chapel_wmk2.jpg' BORDER="0' ALT="2/6' width="116'
height="140">
<img SRC="kings_chapel_wmk3.jpg' BORDER="0' ALT="3/6' width="118'
height="140">
</nobr>
<br>
<nobr>
<img SRC="kings_chapel_wmk4.jpg' BORDER="0' ALT="4/6' width="116'
height="140">
```

```
<img SRC="kings_chapel_wmk5.jpg' BORDER="0' ALT="5/6' width="116'
height="140">
<img SRC="kings_chapel_wmk6.jpg' BORDER="0' ALT="6/6' width="118'
height="140">
</nobr>
```

Issues in Information Hiding

The following three sections discuss issues that must be considered when hiding information.

Level of Visibility

The way a message is embedded will determine whether the data is perceptible or not. To reduce the theft of data, the presence of a watermark is often publicized. However, publicizing the presence of a watermark also allows various methods to be implemented to attempt to alter or disable the watermark. When the visibility of the data is increased, the potential for manipulation of the data also increases.

Robustness Versus Payload

In order to have a robust method of embedding a message, redundancy should be maintained to resist changes made to the cover. However, increasing the robustness of the message means that less space is usable for the payload. Robustness must be weighed against the size of the payload.

File Format Dependence

Conversion of files that have lossless information to compressed files with lossy information can destroy the secret information present in the cover. Some processes embed the data depending on the file format of the carrier, while others do not depend on the file format. The JPEG compression algorithm uses floating-point calculations to translate the picture into an array of integers. This conversion process can result in rounding errors that may eliminate portions of the image. This process does not result in any noticeable difference in the image. Nevertheless, embedded data could become damaged.

Some other popular algorithms, namely, Windows Bitmap (BMP) and Graphic Interchange Format (GIF), are considered lossless compressions. The compressed image is an exact representation of the original.

Detecting Steganography

The following indicators are likely signs of steganography:

- *Software clues on the computer*: The investigator should determine the filenames and Web sites the suspect used by viewing the browser's cookies or history. An investigator should also look in registry key entries, the mailbox of the suspect, chat or instant messaging logs, and communication or comments made by the suspect. Because these data are important for investigation, they give clues to the investigator for further procedures.

- *Other program files*: It is also important to check other program files because it is possible that a nonprogram file may be a cover file that hides other files inside it. The investigator should also check software that is not normally used for steganography such as binary (hex) editors, disk-wiping software, or other software used for changing data from one code to another.

- *Multimedia files*: The investigator should look for large files in the system, as they can be used as carrier files for steganography. If the investigator finds a number of large duplicate files, then it is possible that they are used as carrier files.

Detection Techniques

Detecting steganographic content is difficult, especially when low payloads are used. The following techniques are used for detecting steganography:

- *Statistical tests*: These tests reveal that an image has been modified by examining the statistical properties of the original. Some of the tests are not dependent on the data format and will measure the entropy of the redundant data, so the images with hidden data will have more entropy than the original image.

- *Stegdetect*: Stegdetect is an automated tool that detects the hidden content in images. It detects different steganographic methods for embedding steganographic messages in images.

- *Stegbreak*: Stegbreak breaks the encoding password with the help of dictionary guessing. It can be used in launching dictionary attacks against JSteg-Shell, JPHS, and OutGuess.

- *Visible noise*: Attacks on hidden information can employ detection, extraction, and disabling or damaging hidden information. The images that have large payloads display distortions from the hidden data.

- *Appended spaces and invisible characters*: Using invisible characters or appended spaces is a form of hiding data in the spaces of the text. The presence of many white spaces is an indication of steganography.

- *Color palettes*: Some application characteristics are exclusive to steganography tools. The color palettes used in steganographic programs have unique characteristics. Modifications in the color palettes create a detectable steganographic signature.

Detecting Text, Image, Audio, and Video Steganography

Hidden information is detected in different ways depending on the type of file that is used. The following file types require specific methods to detect hidden messages.

Text Files When a message is hidden in a text file so that the message can be detected only with the knowledge of the secret file, it was probably hidden by altering the cover source. For text files, the alterations are made to the character positions. These alterations can be detected by looking for text patterns or disturbances, the language used, and an unusual number of blank spaces.

Image Files The hidden data in an image can be detected by determining changes in size, file format, last modified time stamp, and color palette of the file.

Statistical analysis methods can be used when scanning an image. Assuming that the least significant bit is more or less random is an incorrect assumption since applying a filter that shows the LSBs can produce a recognizable image. Therefore, it can be concluded that LSBs are not random. Rather, they consist of information about the entire image.

When a secret message is inserted into an image, LSBs are no longer random. With encrypted data that has high entropy, the LSB of the cover will not contain the information about the original and is more or less random. By using statistical analysis on the LSB, the difference between random values and real values can be identified.

Audio Files Statistical analysis methods can be used for audio files since LSB modifications are also used on audio.

The following techniques are also useful for detecting hidden data:

- Scanning information for inaudible frequencies
- Determining odd distortions and patterns that show the existence of secret data

Video Files Detection of secret data in video files includes a combination of the methods used in image and audio files.

Steganalysis Steganalysis is the reverse process of steganography. Steganography hides data, while steganalysis is used to detect hidden data. Steganalysis detects the encoded hidden message and, if possible, recovers that message. The messages are detected by verifying the differences between bit patterns and unusually large file sizes.

Steganalysis Methods/Attacks on Steganography Steganography attacks are categorized by the following seven types:

1. *Stego-only attack*: The stego-only attack takes place when only the stego-medium is used to carry out the attack. The only way to avoid this attack is by detecting and extracting the embedded message.

2. *Known-cover attack*: The known-cover attack is used with the presence of both a stego-medium and a cover medium. The attacker can compare both media and detect the format change.

3. *Known-message attack*: The known-message attack presumes that the message and the stego-medium are present and the technique by which the message was embedded can be determined.

4. *Known-stego attack*: In this attack the steganography algorithm is known, and the original object and the stego-objects are available.

5. *Chosen-stego attack*: The chosen-stego attack takes place when the forensic investigator generates a stego-medium from the message using a special tool.

6. *Chosen-message attack*: The steganalyst obtains a stego-object from a steganography tool or algorithm of a chosen message. This attack is intended to find the patterns in the stego-object that point to the use of specific steganography tools or algorithms.

7. *Disabling or active attacks*: These attacks are categorized into the following six types:

   1) *Blurring*: Blurring attacks can smooth transitions and reduce contrast by averaging the pixels next to the hard edges of defined lines and the areas where there are significant color transitions.

2) *Noise reduction*: Random noise in the stego-medium inserts random-colored pixels into the image. The uniform noise inserts pixels and colors that look similar to the original pixels. Noise reduction decreases the noise in the image by adjusting the colors and averaging the pixel values.

3) *Sharpening*: Sharpening is the opposite of the blurring effect. It increases the contrast between the adjacent pixels where there are significant color contrasts that are usually at the edge of objects.

4) *Rotation*: Rotation moves the stego-medium to give its center a point.

5) *Resampling*: Resampling involves a process known as interpolation. This process is used to reduce the raggedness associated with the stego-medium. It is normally used to resize the image.

6) *Softening*: Softening of the stego-medium applies a uniform blur to an image in order to smooth edges and reduce contrasts. It causes less distortion than blurring.

Stego-Forensics

Stego-forensics is an area of forensic science dealing with steganography techniques to investigate a source or cause of a crime. Different methods of steganalysis can be used to unearth secret communications between antisocial elements and criminals.

Tools

2Mosaic

2Mosaic is a small, command-line utility for Windows that will break apart any JPEG file and generate the HTML code needed to reconstruct the picture.

2Mosaic is a presentation attack against digital watermarking systems. It is of general applicability and possesses the property that allows a marked image to be unmarked and still rendered by a standard browser in exactly the same way as the marked image.

The attack was motivated by an automatic system that was fielded for copyright piracy detection. It consists of a watermarking scheme plus a Web crawler that downloads pictures from the Internet and checks whether they contain a watermark.

It consists of chopping an image up into a number of smaller subimages that are embedded in a suitable sequence in a Web page. Common Web browsers render juxtaposed subimages stuck together, so they appear identical to the original image. This attack appears to be quite general; all marking schemes require the marked image to have some minimal size (one cannot hide a meaningful mark in just one pixel). Thus, by splitting an image into sufficiently small pieces, the mark detector will be confused. The best that one can hope for is that the minimal size could be quite small, rendering the method impractical.

BlindSide

The BlindSide tool can hide files of any file type within a Windows bitmap image. The original and the encoded image look identical to the human eye. However, when the image is executed through BlindSide, the concealed data can be extracted and retrieved. For added security, the data can be scrambled with a password so that no one will be able to access the data. The BlindSide tool analyzes color differentials in an image so that it will only alter pixels it knows will not be noticeable to the human eye. The main limitation to BlindSide is that each image has its own capability that is dependent on color patterns within it.

The BlindSide tool can be used in many ways. The main advantage of BlindSide is that it uses a steganographic technique, supplemented with a cryptographic algorithm. This means that one can pass messages without arousing suspicion. BlindSide allows the user to encrypt messages with a password-based encryption so that even if someone did examine these images, they would need a password to obtain the secret data. Digital publishers typically use BlindSide to embed a license file and copyright notice within the images that are to be published. A similar procedure could be applied to images on a company's Web pages.

S-Tools

The S-Tools steganographic tool has the ability to hide multiple files within a single object. S-Tools first compresses the individual files, which are stored with their names, and then it inserts filler on the front of the data to prevent two identical sets of files from encrypting in the same way. All files are then encrypted using the passphrase that the user generates. The encryption algorithms operate in cipher-feedback mode. The S-Tools application seeds a cryptographically strong, pseudorandom number from the passphrase and uses its output to choose the position of the next bit from the cover data to be used.

For example, if a sound file had 100 bits available for hiding and the user wanted to use 10 of those bits to hold a message, S-Tools would not choose bits zero through nine as they are easily detected by a potential enemy. Instead, it might choose bits 63, 32, 89, 2, 53, 21, 35, 44, 99, and 80.

StegHide

StegHide is a steganography tool that is able to hide information in images and audio files. The color and frequencies are not changed during the embedding process. Features of this tool include compression of the embedded data, encryption of the embedded information, and automatic integrity checking using a checksum. JPEG, BMP, and WAV file formats are supported for use as a cover file. No such restrictions are imposed on the format of the secret data.

StegHide also uses the graph-theoretic approach to steganography. The investigator does not need to know anything about graph theory to use the StegHide application. The following steps illustrate the working of an embedding algorithm:

1. The secret information is compressed and encrypted.

2. Based on a pseudorandom number, a sequence of pixel positions, which is initialized with a passphrase, is created.

3. By using a graph-theoretic matching algorithm, the application finds pairs of positions so that exchanging their values has the effect of embedding the information.

4. The pixels at the remaining positions are also modified to contain the embedded information. The default encryption algorithm is Rijndael, with a key size of 128 bits in the cipher block-chaining mode.

Snow

Snow is a steganography tool that exploits the nature of white space. It achieves this by appending white space to the end of lines in ASCII text to conceal messages. White-space steganography can be detected by applications such as Word.

Snow is susceptible to this factor. The basic assumption of Snow is that spaces and tabs are generally not visible in text viewers and therefore, a message can be effectively hidden without affecting the text's visual representation from the casual observer. Encryption is provided using the Information Concealment Engine (ICE) encryption algorithm in one-bit cipher-feedback (CFB) mode. Because of ICE's arbitrary key size, passwords of any length up to 1,170 characters are supported. Snow takes advantage of the fact that, since trailing spaces and tabs occasionally occur naturally, their existence will not be sufficient to immediately alert an observer who may stumble across them.

The Snow program runs in two modes: message concealment and message extraction. The data are concealed in the text file by appending sequences of up to seven spaces, interspersed with tabs. This usually allows three bits to be stored every eight columns. The start of the data is indicated by an appended tab character, which allows the insertion of e-mail and news headers without corrupting the data. Snow provides rudimentary compression, using Huffman tables optimized for English text. However, if the data are not text, or if there is a lot of data, the use of an external compression program such as compress or gzip is recommended. If a message string or message file is specified on the command line, Snow attempts to conceal the message in the file <infile>, or standard input otherwise. The resulting file is written to <outfile> if specified, or standard output if not specified. If no message string is provided, Snow attempts to extract a message from the input file. The result is written to the output file or standard output.

Camera/Shy

Camera/Shy is a simple steganography tool that allows users to encrypt information and hide it in standard GIF images. What makes this program different from most steganography tools is its ease of use, making it a desirable component of a cracker's arsenal.

While other steganography programs are command-line based, Camera/Shy is embedded in a Web browser. Other programs require users to know beforehand that an image contains embedded content. Camera/Shy, however, allows users to check images for embedded messages, read them, and embed their own return messages with the click of a mouse.

The Camera/Shy program allows Internet users to conceal information, viruses, or exploitative software inside graphics files on Web pages. Camera/Shy bypasses most known monitoring methods. Utilizing LSB steganographic techniques and AES 256-bit encryption, this application enables users to share censored information with their friends by hiding it in plain view as an ordinary GIF image. Moreover, it leaves no trace on the user's system. It allows a user to make a Web site C/S-enabled (Camera/Shy-enabled) and allows a reader to decrypt images from an HTML page on the fly.

Steganos

Steganos is a steganography tool that combines cryptography and steganography to hide information. It first encrypts the information and then hides it with steganographic techniques. With the help of Steganos the user can store a file with a copyright and prove ownership of a picture if someone tries to use it.

Steganos can hide a file inside a BMP, VOC, WAV, or ASCII file.

Gifshuffle

Gifshuffle hides messages inside GIF images by mixing up the colors within the images so that it is difficult to find the original message. It supports GIF images that have features such as transparency and animation. Gifshuffle compresses the message using Huffman tables. If there is a lot of data or the data does not contain text, then a gzip compression program is used. The message also gets encrypted using the ICE encryption algorithm in the one-bit CFB mode. ICE supports arbitrary keys and passwords of any length.

For example, to hide the message "eccouncil is best" in the file ecc.gif with compression and encryption using the password "eccouncil," the following command should be used:

gifshuffle -C -m "eccouncil is best" -p "eccouncil" ecc.gif outfile.gif

To extract the message, the following command should be used:

gifshuffle -C -p "eccouncil" outfile.gif

The following syntax is used in the commands:

- -C: Compress the data if concealing, or uncompress it if extracting
- -m: message string; the contents of this string will be concealed in the input GIF image.
- -p: password; with this password, data will be encrypted during concealment and decrypted during extraction.

JPHS

JPHS hides files in JPEG format. For a typical visual image and a low insertion rate of up to 5 percent, it is nearly impossible for someone to detect that a JPEG file processed with this tool contains hidden data.

OutGuess

OutGuess is a steganography tool that inserts hidden information into redundant bits of data sources. During extraction, the redundant bits are extracted and written back after modification. OutGuess supports PNM and JPEG images. In the JPEG format, OutGuess maintains statistics based on frequency counts. Before hiding the data, OutGuess determines the size of the hidden data and maintains the statistics. Due to this, statistical tests based on frequency counts are unable to detect the presence of steganographic content.

The following example is of the data embedding procedure:

outguess -k "my secret key" -d hidden.txt demo.jpg out.jpg

Reading demo.jpg....

JPEG compression quality set to 75

Extracting usable bits: 40,059 bits

Correctable message size: 21,194 bits, 52.91%

Encoded 'snark.bz2': 14,712 bits, 1839 bytes

Finding best embedding...

0: 7467(50.6%)[50.8%], bias 8137(1.09), saved: 13, total: 18.64%

1: 7311(49.6%)[49.7%], bias 8079(1.11), saved: 5, total: 18.25%

4: 7250(49.2%)[49.3%], bias 7906(1.09), saved: -13, total: 18.10%

59: 7225(49.0%)[49.1%], bias 7889(1.09), saved: 16, total: 18.04%

59, 7225: Embedding data: 14,712 in 40,059

Bits embedded: 14,744, changed: 7225(49.0%)[49.1%], bias: 7889, tot: 40,032, skip: 25,288

Foiling statistics: corrections: 2590, failed: 1, offset: 122.585494 +- 239.664983

Total bits changed: 15,114 (change 7225 + bias 7889)

Storing bitmap into data...

Writing foil/out.jpg....

The following example is of the data extraction procedure:

outguess -k "my secret key" -r out.jpg hidden.txt

Reading out.jpg....

Extracting usable bits: 40,059 bits

Steg retrieve: seed: 7225, len: 1839

Invisible Secrets 4

Invisible Secrets 4 supports both cryptography and steganography. It first encrypts the message and then hides it behind a variety of files. The user can directly encrypt and hide files from Windows Explorer and transfer them over the Internet via e-mail. Invisible Secrets 4 can hide information behind JPEG, PNG, BMP, HTML, and WAV files.

Invisible Secrets 4 includes the following features:

- Helps to hide files, encrypt files, destroy Internet traces, shred files, make secure IP-to-IP password transfers, and even lock any application on a computer
- Allows data compression before the encrypt/hide process
- Uses strong file-encryption algorithms, including Rijndael Advanced Encryption Standard (AES)
- Supports password management solutions that store all passwords
- Supports a shredder that destroys files, folders, and Internet traces beyond recovery
- Has a locker that allows password protection for certain applications
- Creates self-decrypting packages that can be mailed over the Internet
- Helps transfer passwords securely over the Internet

Masker

Masker provides strong security for data. It encrypts files and hides those files behind image, video, program, or sound files. It provides up to 448-bit encryption and password protection. The cover file remains functional. This means that if it is a sound or video file, it can be played without trouble.

Masker includes the following features:

- Hides files, folders, and subfolders within a carrier file
- Reveals and extracts hidden files and folders from a carrier file

- Encryption (up to 448 bits) and compression
- Seven strong encryption algorithms (Blowfish, Rijndael, etc.) are available
- Supports multiple hideouts
- Preview function (hidden files can be previewed and modified in hidden mode)
- Search function
- Lock/unlock function blocks unauthorized use

Data Stash

Data Stash (Figure 1-7) is a steganography tool that hides sensitive data files behind other files. With this tool the user can use any large bitmap or database file as the cover file and select the files to be hidden by using the drag-and-drop function. In this method the carrier file remains active. This tool supports password protection, with the help of Blowfish encryption.

Source: http://www.skyjuicesoftware.com/images/screenshots/ds_main.gif

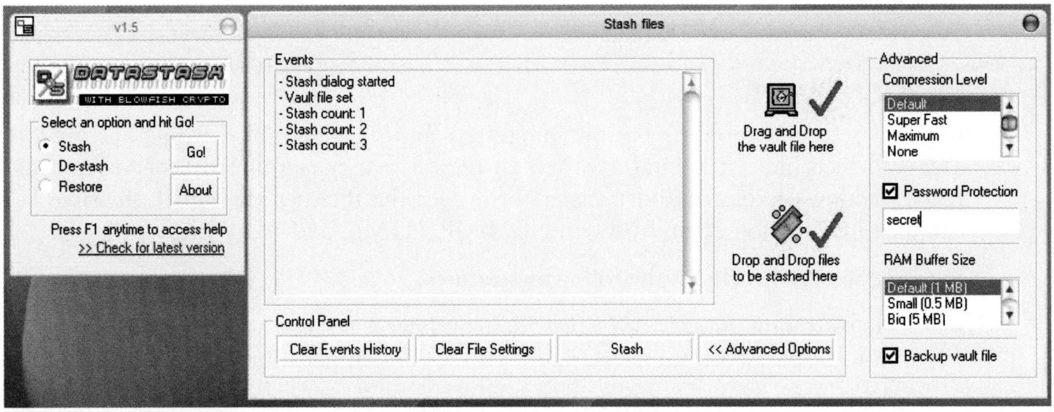

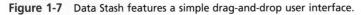

Figure 1-7 Data Stash features a simple drag-and-drop user interface.

Data Stash includes the following features:

- Hides files within files
- Receptacle file remains fully functional
- Supports a wide variety of file formats (MPEG, JPEG, MP3, EXE, COM, etc.)
- Password protection using Blowfish encryption
- Fast operation

StegaNote

The StegaNote tool uses cryptosecure steganography that mixes up the compressed file and text from a text editor with the cover file, rendering it invisible to the human eye. This tool hides data in image files. It uses the RPP (random pixel positioning) technique, making it impossible to extract the original data. RPP uses a pseudorandom number generator (PRNG) in feedback mode, and starts with the key or password, which contains a series of coordinates to detect the pixels used to hold the data. This spreads data over the cover image. The data bits are stored into the LSB of the colors red, green, and blue. The main use of the RPP is to protect data against cryptanalysis. It has an easy and clear user interface.

Stegomagic

Stegomagic is a steganography tool that uses text, WAV, 24-bit BMP, and 256-color BMP files to hide data. The size of the cover file remains the same except in the case of text files. Data is encrypted and protected with a password using the DES algorithm and it is subsequently hidden behind the cover file. It supports all Microsoft Windows environments.

Hermetic Stego

The Hermetic Stego tool hides data files in either a single image or a set of BMP images. The data file may be of any type and size. It hides the data with or without a key. Hermetic Stego has the following features:

- It can hide data of any type and any size.
- The bits of data are inserted into the bytes of image files, making it impossible to crack.
- Data can be transported with or without the stego-key, which encrypts the data.

A user takes the following steps to hide data files:

- Select the data file to be hidden.
- Enter the stego-key.
- Select the image files in which to hide the data and the input image file folder that contains the BMP images for hiding the data.
- Specify the folder to receive the stego images; this is known as the Stego images folder.

StegParty

StegParty is a system for hiding information inside plaintext files. Unlike similar tools currently available, it does not use random gibberish to encode data. Instead, it relies on small alterations, like changes in spelling and punctuation, to the message. StegParty also does not, by default, use white space to encode data. This is because white-space-encoded messages are too easy to detect, and too easy to alter in a way that would destroy the encoded message. But since StegParty is customizable, features can be added.

Stego Suite

Stego Suite is a tool that identifies the presence of steganography without prior knowledge of the steganography algorithm that might have been used against the target file. This is known as blind steganography detection.

Stego Suite's tools provide the ability to quickly examine and evaluate digital images and/or audio data for the presence of hidden information or communications. It comprises the following four tools:

- StegoHunter
- StegoWatch

- StegoAnalyst
- StegoBreak

StegoHunter StegoHunter is designed to quickly, accurately, and easily detect steganography programs as a first step in the investigation process. With Stego Hunter, results are easily reported to the investigator of any installed or even previously installed applications. The suspected carrier types are flagged to further the investigation process. Forensic images of other popular forensic tools such as EnCase, FTK, dd, and Safeback can be scanned.

StegoWatch StegoWatch allows users to detect digital steganography and can use a dictionary attack to extract information that has been embedded with some of the most popular steganography tools.

StegoAnalyst StegoAnalyst is a full-featured imaging and analysis tool. It allows investigators to search for visual clues that steganography has, in fact, been utilized in both image and audio files. A file viewing panel is provided that displays the individual file image or audio wave and the file attributes, including image details, DCT coefficients, and color pairs. In order to allow investigators to look for further clues that steganography is in use, filter options are included that transform the images into one of three different presentations: intensity, saturation, or hue. Other filter options display only selected LSBs of specific colors. Since many steganographic techniques use LSBs for data hiding, viewing the LSBs of an image can sometimes reveal indicators of steganography.

StegoBreak StegoBreak is a built-in utility designed to obtain the passphrase that has been used on a file found to contain steganography. Included with the purchase of the tool are popular password dictionaries used to execute a dictionary attack. Investigators also have the ability to bring in other dictionaries. Alternately, if they have obtained the password through suspect questioning, they can run the password against the detected image or audio files.

StegSpy

StegSpy detects steganography and the program used to hide the message. It also identifies the location of the hidden content. StegSpy currently identifies the following programs:

- Hiderman
- JPHS
- Masker
- Invisible Secrets

WNSTORM

WNSTORM is used to encrypt files to keep prying eyes from invading a user's privacy. It can hide files within PCX images. WNSTORM's method of hiding files in PCX images is very secure. A user can take the PCX image containing the hidden data and send it to any source. Only the sender and the one whom the password is shared with can get at the hidden data file.

Xidie

Xidie enables the user to hide and encrypt files within other files. It can encrypt sensitive information while simultaneously hiding it in a file that will not look suspicious. The carrier files are fully functional and almost identical to the original files.

Options like encrypt and burn, hide and burn, encrypt and mail, and hide and mail make the work easier. The program directly transfers archives through the use of an FTP module.

CryptArkan

CryptArkan encrypts and hides data files and directories inside one or more container files. Hidden data can be directly read off an audio CD.

CryptArkan performs the following functions:

- Encrypts data files to be hidden
- Hides data files in multiple container files
- Can hide whole directories, preserving subdirectory structure
- Can use different hiding methods for separate container files
- Uses different amounts of the original container file for data

Stealth Files

Stealth Files is a tool that takes a PGP 2.x encrypted message and strips any standard headers off to ensure that the result looks like random noise. If the Pretty Good Privacy (PGP) random number generators are secure, and if International Data Encryption Algorithm (IDEA) and Rivest-Shamir-Adleman (RSA) (RSA when normalized) produce good-quality random numbers, the result should look like white noise and stand up to analysis as being indistinguishable from white noise. Stealth Files can also be used to produce random numbers.

Camouflage

Camouflage allows the user to hide files by scrambling them and then attaching them to a carrier file. A camouflaged file behaves like a normal file and can be stored, used, or e-mailed without attracting attention. It can be password protected for additional security.

CryptoBola JPEG

CryptoBola JPEG stores only the ciphertext without any additional information like filename, type, or length. It determines which parts (bits) of the JPEG-encoded data play the least significant role in the reproduction of the image and replaces those bits with the bits of the ciphertext. The plaintext can be any data file or it can be entered in edit mode directly before the actual embedding takes place.

Steganosaurus

Steganosaurus is a plaintext steganography utility that encodes a (usually encrypted) binary file as gibberish text. The encoding is based on either a spelling dictionary or words taken from a text document.

Chapter Summary

- Steganography is the method of hiding information by embedding the message into a seemingly harmless message.

- Cryptography is the technique of encoding the contents of a message in such a way that its contents are hidden from outsiders. Here, existence of the message is clear but the meaning is obscured.

- Watermarking is used for authentication and copyright protection.

- Steganalysis is a technique used to detect and extract hidden data.

- Steganography is used for secure and secret communication.

- Data Stash is a security tool that allows the user to hide sensitive data files within other files.

- Stegomagic hides any kind of file or message in text, WAV, 24-bit BMP, and 256-color BMP files.

Key Terms

cover medium	steganography	stegosystem
digital watermark	stego-key	
least significant bit (LSB)	stego-medium	

Review Questions

1. Define steganography.

_____

_____

_____

_____

2. What is a watermark?

_____

_____

_____

_____

3. How is steganography different from cryptography?

_____

_____

_____

_____

4. Name the three main types of steganography.

_____

_____

_____

_____

5. How is steganography used with audio files?

_____

_____

_____

_____

6. What is a cover medium?

_____

_____

_____

_____

7. Name two legal uses for steganography.

_____

_____

_____

_____

8. Explain the least-significant-bit method of steganography.

_____

_____

_____

_____

9. Name two technical methods used to embed messages in a text file.

_____

_____

_____

_____

10. Explain the process of echo data hiding.

_____

_____

_____

_____

Hands-On Projects

HANDS-ON PROJECTS

1. Review steganography tools:
   • Pick three steganography tools mentioned in this chapter to review.
   • Identify and compare the features of each tool. Identify no less than 5 comparison points.
   • Prepare a table detailing the results of your research.

2. Evaluate a steganography tool:
   • Pick one of the steganography tools mentioned in this chapter to evaluate.
   • Download and install the tool.
   • Test the tool by using it to perform the function it is designed for.
   • Prepare a one-paragraph summary of your evaluation process.

3. Use Hex Workshop to perform bit-shifting to change the order of binary data, making the data unreadable:
   • Using your preferred Internet browser, navigate to *http://www.bpsoft.com/downloads/* and download and install the latest version of Hex Workshop.
   • Create a .txt file containing the following text: **Secrets are contained in this message. Do not tell anyone the secrets.**
   • Save as secret.txt
   • Start Hex Workshop, open secret.txt

- Click the "Data Operations" command on the toolbar (Figure 1-8) and select "Shift Left" (Figure 1-9).

Figure 1-8   Hex Workshop "Data Operations" command

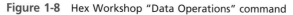

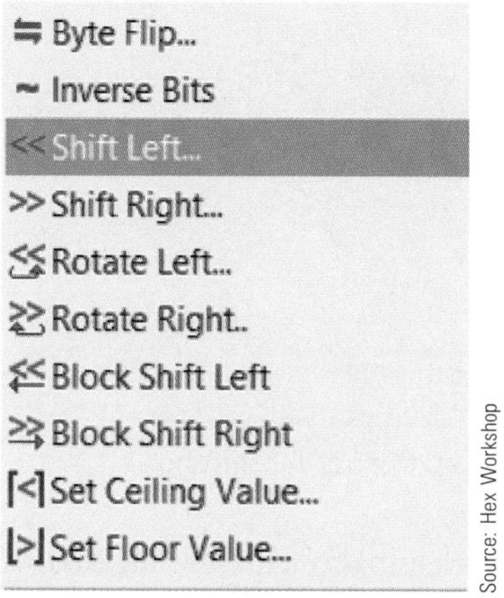

Figure 1-9   Hex Workshop "Shift Left" command.

- Click "OK" to accept the default settings (Figure 1-10).

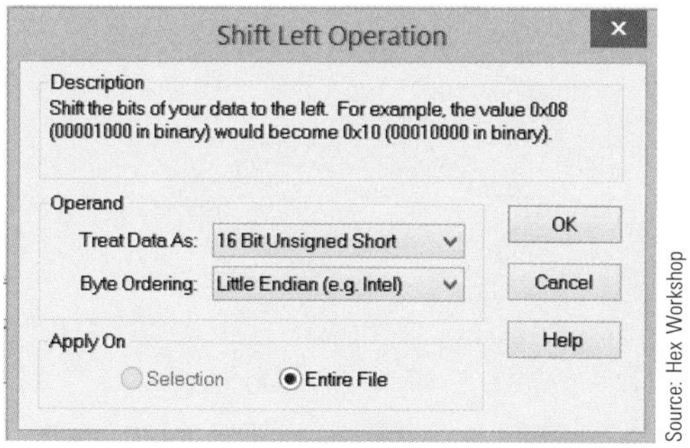

Figure 1-10   Hex Workshop "Shift Left Operation" window.

- Save the new file as secretshifted.txt
- Examine secret.txt before bit-shifting (Figure 1-11):

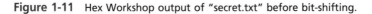

	0	1	2	3	4	5	6	7	8	9	A	0123456789A
00000000	53	65	63	72	65	74	73	20	61	72	65	Secrets are
0000000B	20	63	6F	6E	74	61	69	6E	65	64	20	contained
00000016	69	6E	20	74	68	69	73	20	6D	65	73	in this mes
00000021	73	61	67	65	2E	20	44	6F	20	6E	6F	sage. Do no
0000002C	74	20	74	65	6C	6C	20	61	6E	79	6F	t tell anyo
00000037	6E	65	20	74	68	65	20	73	65	63	72	ne the secr
00000042	65	74	73	2E								ets.

Source: Hex Workshop

Figure 1-11 Hex Workshop output of "secret.txt" before bit-shifting.

- Examine secretshifted.txt after bit-shifting (Figure 1-12):

	0	1	2	3	4	5	6	7	8	9	A	0123456789A
00000000	A6	CA	C6	E4	CA	E8	E6	40	C2	E4	CA	.......@...
0000000B	40	C6	DE	DC	E8	C2	D2	DC	CA	C8	40	@.........@
00000016	D2	DC	40	E8	D0	D2	E6	40	DA	CA	E6	..@....@...
00000021	E6	C2	CE	CA	5C	40	88	DE	40	DC	DE	....\@..@..
0000002C	E8	40	E8	CA	D8	D8	40	C2	DC	F2	DE	.@....@....
00000037	DC	CA	40	E8	D0	CA	40	E6	CA	C6	E4	..@...@....
00000042	CA	E8	E6	5C								...\

Source: Hex Workshop

Figure 1-12 Hex Workshop output of "secretshifted.txt" after bit-shifting.

- Use Hex Workshop (Tools, Generate Checksum) to generate an MD5 Checksum of secret.txt and secretshifted.txt.
- Prepare a one-paragraph summary detailing the results of the two checksums and whether or not you expected them to be the same or different, and why.

chapter 2

Data Acquisition and Duplication

After completing this chapter, you should be able to:

- Determine the best data acquisition methods
- Understand data recovery contingencies
- Understand the need for data duplication
- Use common data acquisition tools
- Use common data duplication tools

What If?

Read back through the Jeremy Johnson case from Chapter 1. Assuming the case is still active, provide answers to the following questions:

- How did Johnson try to hide his images?
- What other methods could he have used to try to hide his wrongdoing?

Introduction to Data Acquisition and Duplication

This chapter focuses on data acquisition and data duplication. **Data acquisition** is the act of taking possession of or obtaining control of data and adding it to a collection of evidence. **Data duplication** is the act of making a copy of data already acquired to preserve the original evidence in pristine condition. The chapter starts by discussing how to determine the best data acquisition methods for a certain situation. It then discusses how to make sure crucial data is not lost during the acquisition process. The chapter then covers the importance of data duplication before moving on to descriptions of the tools investigators use for data acquisition and duplication.

Determining the Best Acquisition Methods

Forensic investigators can acquire digital evidence using the following methods:

1. Creating a bitstream disk-to-image file
2. Making a bitstream disk-to-disk copy
3. Creating a sparse data copy of a folder or file

Disk-to-Image File

Creating a bitstream disk-to-image file is the most common method forensic investigators use. When using this method, forensic investigators are able to make as many copies of the digital evidence as they need. Investigators are able to image the original disk to another disk. An investigator can then make use of other tools such as EnCase, Forensic Toolkit Imager (FTK), Smart, Task, and Ilook to read and analyze the image file.

Disk-to-Disk Copy

If an investigator is unable to create a bitstream disk-to-image file, the alternative is to create a bitstream disk-to-disk copy of the suspect's disk drive in order to acquire the information from it. There are several bitstreaming programs that can copy the information from one disk to another. Disk-to-disk imaging tools include SafeBack, SnapCopy, and Norton Ghost. Many of these applications run under MS-DOS.

Sparse Data Copy

There are times during a forensic investigation when an investigator finds incriminating evidence in a particular file or folder. Therefore, it would not be necessary to create a bitstream disk-to-image file or a disk-to-disk copy. The investigator would just need to create a sparse data copy of the folder or file. A **sparse data copy** is a copy that an investigator makes of only part of a large set of data in which only the data pertinent to the investigation is included. An investigator may choose to make a sparse data copy to reduce the overall size of an evidence file.

Data Recovery Contingencies

Investigators must make contingency plans when data acquisition failure occurs. To preserve digital evidence, investigators must create a duplicate copy of the evidence files. In case the original data recovered is corrupted, investigators can make use of the second copy. Investigators can use forensic tools such as EnCase and SafeBack to obtain multiple copies.

Typically, computer forensic investigators make at least bitstream image copies of the digital evidence that is collected. Investigators have at their disposal more than one bitstreaming tool. They should use at least two of these tools to make copies of the digital evidence in case one tool does not properly acquire the data.

During the data recovery process, an investigator must remember not to make any changes to the digital evidence. Forensic activities must be performed only on the bitstream copies of digital evidence to ensure that the original evidence is not altered or corrupted.

The Need for Data Duplication

Investigators need to be concerned about destructive devices that can be planted in computer systems by their owners. Evidence can be destroyed if an investigator is not careful. These destructive devices can overwrite data fragments, and they can alter or destroy data stored in the Windows swap file. A suspect could use a self-destructing program that could wipe out any evidence when it detects a certain trigger. This can hamper an investigation and make the collection of evidence much more difficult. Thus, data duplication is essential for the proper preservation of digital evidence.

Data Acquisition Software Tools

There are many different data acquisition tools available to forensic investigators. All of these tools have different features that make them useful in different situations.

Windows Standard Tools

Windows data acquisition tools—such as xcopy, diskcopy, Volume Shadow Copy, and Windows Explorer—allow an investigator to easily examine or acquire evidence from a disk with the help of removable media, such as a USB storage device. These tools can also use

Firewire to connect hard disks to forensic lab systems. However, Windows data acquisition tools cannot acquire data from a protected area of a disk.

Windows is equipped with many tools that are intended for administrators but are also useful for computer forensic investigators. These tools permit the investigator to acquire and replicate digital evidence. The forensic investigator is able to find out where logical volume information is found and is able to collect evidence from a system even when it is running. Windows data acquisition tools enable forensic investigators to acquire a full logical image of a drive. But, Windows tools can only acquire data that the operating system can recognize and do not include slack space or deleted files.

Home and workplace computer systems are designed with hard drives with large storage capacities. Imaging a 500 GB hard drive using traditional methods, for instance, may take a total of 24 hours to complete. From a forensic investigative point of view, 24 hours is a long time. This can lead to a loss of productivity for the company that owns the computer containing the evidence.

On the other hand, data acquisition programs like dd and netcat usually spend a lot of time copying data from one buffer to another. In order to image a logical volume, data on the volume must be paged from internal buffers to the file systems in memory. This process takes a lot of time, and this is one of the main limitations of standard forensic tools when compared to Windows forensic tools.

Linux Standard Tools

Forensic investigators use the built-in Linux command dd to copy data from a disk drive. This command can make a bitstream disk-to-disk copy or a disk-to-image file. The dd command can copy data from any disk that Linux can mount and access. Other forensic tools, such as AccessData FTK and Ilook, can read dd image files.

One of the advantages of using the dd command in Linux is that it is free software that does not rely on any additional resources from the computer. The dd command in Linux can create images of ext2, ext3, UNIX, FAT12, FAT16, FAT32, NTFS, HFS, and HPFS file-system disks. The dd command also enables examiners to extract digital evidence and copy it to any type of media that the Linux operating system is able to access.

The dd command in Linux does have certain limitations. An investigator needs to understand and be able to implement advanced UNIX shell scripting commands. The investigator must also define the exact number of blocks in the save set volume in order to create a volume save set. Also, the dd command is not available in all versions of Linux.

Using the dd Command   The syntax for the dd command is as follows:

dd if=<source> of=<target> bs=<byte size> (usually some power of 2, not less than 512 bytes [i.e., 512, 1024, 2048, 4096, 8192]) **skip= seek= conv=<conversion>**

- *source*: where the data is to be read from
- *target*: where the data is to be written to
- *skip*: number of blocks to skip at start of input

- *seek*: number of blocks to skip at start of output
- *conv*: conversion options

For example, an investigator would use the following commands for these tasks:

- To make a complete physical backup of a hard disk:
  dd if=/dev/hda of=/dev/case5img1
- To copy one hard disk partition to another hard disk:
  dd if=/dev/sda2 of=/dev/sdb2 bs=4096 conv=notrunc,noerror
- To make an image of a CD:
  dd if=/dev/hdc of=/home/sam/mycd.iso bs=2048 conv=notrunc
- To copy a floppy disk:
  dd if=/dev/fd0 of=/home/sam/floppy.image conv=notrunc
- To restore a disk partition from an image file:
  dd if=/home/sam/partition.image of=/dev/sdb2 bs=4096 conv=notrunc,noerror
- To copy RAM memory to a file:
  dd if=/dev/mem of=/home/sam/mem.bin bs=1024

Using dd to Extract the MBR

The master boot record (MBR) is the consistent starting point for hard disks. It stores information about the disk. The MBR is always located at cylinder zero, head zero, and sector one, the first sector on the disk.

The MBR consists of the following:

- *Master partition table*: This table contains a complete description of the partitions on the disk.
- *Master boot code*: This is the small bit of code that the BIOS loads to start the bootstrapping process.

To see the contents of the MBR, an investigator uses the following commands:

dd if=/dev/hda of=mbr.bin bs=512 count=1

od -xa mbr.bin

This dd command must be run as root. It reads the first 512 bytes from /dev/hda (the first Integrated Drive Electronics (IDE) drive) and writes them to the mbr.bin file.

The od command prints the binary file in hex and ASCII formats.

Using netcat with dd

The netcat command supports the dd command with networking features. An investigator can use it to read and write data across the network using TCP or UDP. **TCP** is a protocol that implements a core set of rules that allow reliable connection-oriented connections between host computers over a network. **UDP** is a nonreliable protocol that implements a best-effort set of rules that allow for network communication where exact delivery of each packet is not critical, such as for streaming video.

To make a partition image on another machine:

- On a source machine:

  dd if=/dev/hda bs=16065b | netcat targethost-IP 1234

- On a target machine:

  netcat -l -p 1234 | dd of=/dev/hdc bs=16065b

DriveSpy

DriveSpy enables an investigator to direct information from one particular sector range to another sector. The DriveSpy application gives forensic investigators two methods to access disk sectors:

1. Defining the absolute starting sector after a command and the total number of sectors to be read on the drive

2. Listing the absolute starting and ending sectors

Many of the DriveSpy commands are able to work with multiple ranges of sectors. These commands include CopySect, SaveSect, WriteSect, and Wipe. When a sector range is required as a parameter for a DriveSpy command, the ranges may be specified using the following syntax:

   [Drive ID]: [Absolute Start Sector],[Number of Sectors]
   [Drive ID]: [Absolute Start Sector]-[Absolute End Sector]

An investigator specifies the exact sector range by identifying a starting sector and then the total number of sectors using the first syntax. The second syntax defines a range by identifying both the starting and ending sectors. A comma and a hyphen differentiate the two syntaxes.

DriveSpy Data Manipulation Commands
There are two commands in DriveSpy that are used for data manipulation:

1. *SaveSect*: The SaveSect command is used to copy particular sectors on a disk to a file. The SaveSect command copies the sectors as a bitstream image so that the file is a duplicate of the original sectors. The syntax for the SaveSect command is as follows:

   SAVESECT [Source Sector Range] [Destination File]

   If a path is not identified in the file specification, the file is created in the current working directory.

2. *WriteSect*: The WriteSect command is used to regenerate information acquired through the SaveSect command. The WriteSect command copies the contents of an image file created by SaveSect to a series of sectors. The syntax for the WriteSect command is as follows:

   WRITESECT [Source File] [Destination Sector Range]

   As with the SaveSect command, if a path is not identified in the file specification, the file is created in the current working directory.

DriveSpy Data Preservation Commands The DriveSpy application gives forensic examiners the ability to create and restore compressed images of drive partitions. If an investigator makes an image of a DOS partition, the free space is not included, as DOS cannot see the free space in a cluster. However, if an investigator makes an image of a non-DOS partition, every byte is preserved, including the free space.

There are three data preservation commands available in DriveSpy:

1. *SavePart*: The main function of the SavePart command is to generate an image of a partition. The syntax of the SavePart command is as follows:

    SAVEPART [Destination File]

    Investigators mainly make use of the SavePart command in DriveSpy to create a compressed forensic image of the present partition. SavePart allows an investigator to span media to store the complete image when necessary. After creating an image of the partition, DriveSpy provides a summary of the MD5 hash that is maintained for the image to ensure data integrity when the image is restored.

2. *WritePart*: The main function of the WritePart command is to restore an image of a partition. The image can be one that is stored in the partition that is being examined. The syntax of the WritePart command is as follows:

    WRITEPART [Source File]

    If the image is stored across many parts of media, the WritePart command would automatically look for the media that is necessary.

3. *CopySect*: The main function of the CopySect command is to copy sectors from one disk to a location on the same disk or on a different disk. The syntax of the CopySect command is as follows:

    COPYSECT [Source Sector Range] [Destination Sector Range]

    Forensic investigators most often use the CopySect command as it helps in creating direct disk-to-disk images of suspect media.

FTK Imager

The Forensic Toolkit Imager (FTK Imager) is a commercial forensic imaging software package distributed by AccessData.

FTK Imager allows a forensic investigator to acquire physical device images and logically view data from FAT, NTFS, ext2, ext3, HFS, and HFS+ file systems. Figure 2-1 shows the main FTK Imager screen.

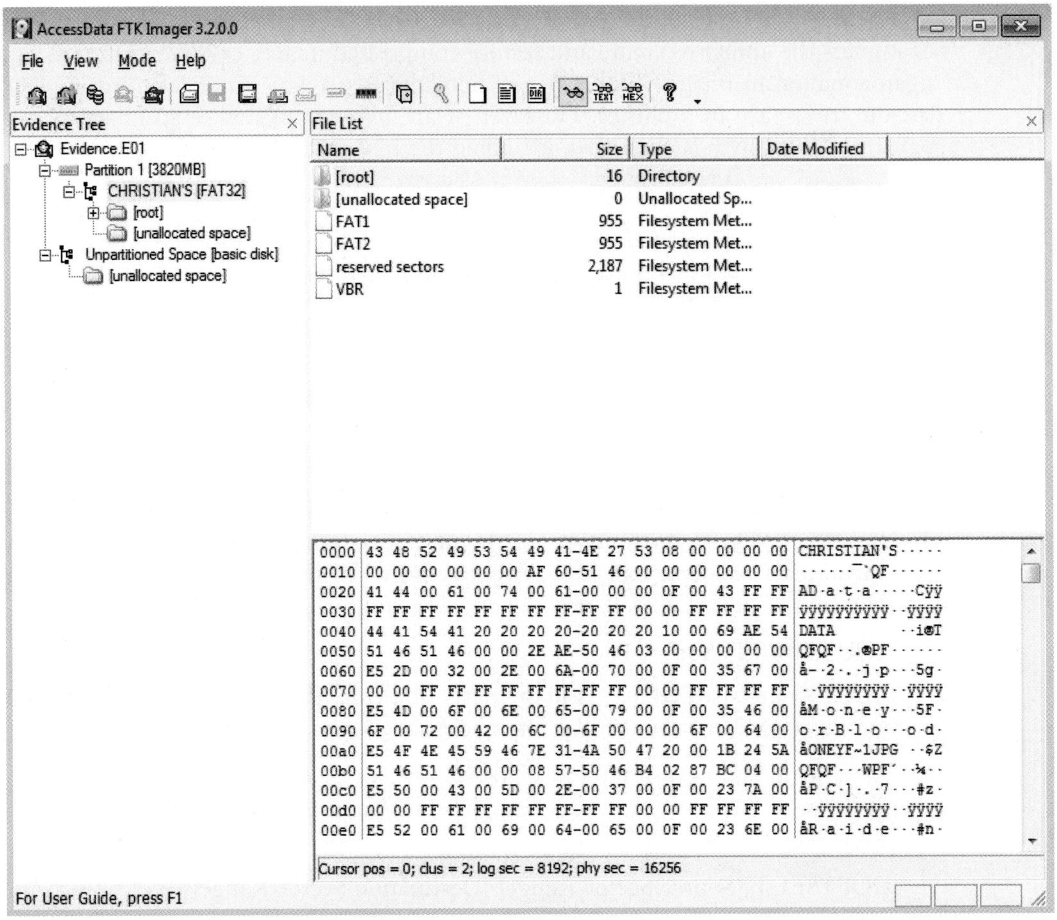

Figure 2-1 FTK Imager is a powerful data acquisition tool.

Source: FTK Imager 3.2.0.0

Mount Image Pro

Mount Image Pro is a computer forensics tool that allows an investigator to mount the following types of images:

- EnCase
- UNIX/Linux dd
- SMART
- ISO

Key Features of Mount Image Pro The following are the key features of Mount Image Pro:

- It maps an image as a single drive letter so that an investigator can explore unused or unpartitioned disk space or map specific drive letters to any or all partitions within the image files. Figure 2-2 shows an image selection screen in Mount Image Pro.

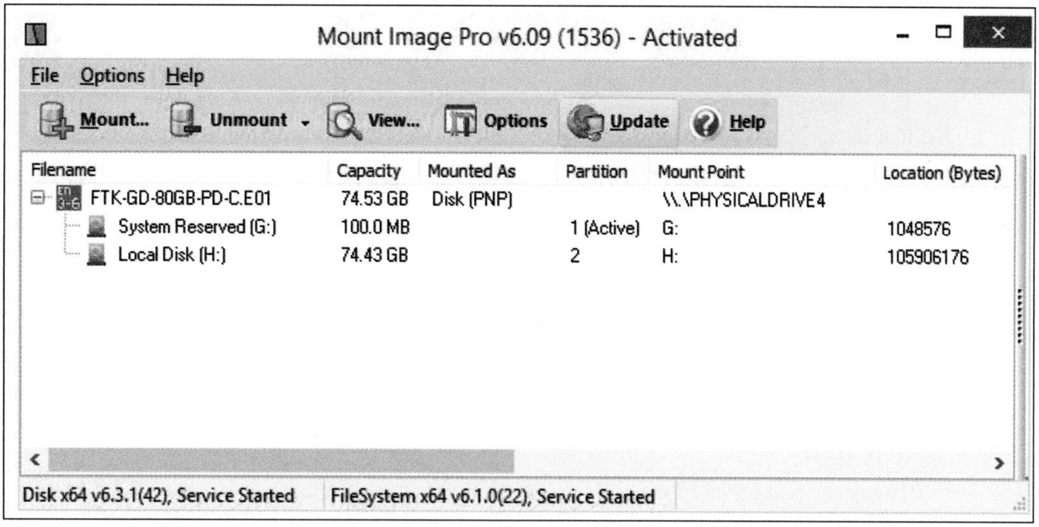

Source: http://www.mountimage.com/encase-mount-screenshots.php

Figure 2-2 An investigator can examine the properties of an image in Mount Image Pro.

- It fully maintains MD5 hash integrity.
- It will open EnCase password-protected image files without the password.
- It is compatible with third-party file-system drivers for Linux.

System Requirements for Mount Image Pro The following are the system requirements for Mount Image Pro:

- *Operating system*: Windows NT/2000/XP/2003/Vista/7/8/10
- *RAM*: 128 MB recommended
- *Hard disk*: At least 6 MB of free disk space

Drive SnapShot

Drive SnapShot is a data acquisition tool that creates an exact disk image. It can create this image while an investigator continues doing his or her work in Windows. Booting into DOS is not necessary. It is compatible with all Windows file systems and most Linux file systems. Only a user with administrative privileges can use Drive SnapShot.

System Requirements for Drive SnapShot

- *Operating system*: Windows NT/2000/XP/2003/Vista/7/8/10
- *RAM*: 8 MB
- *Hard disk*: At least 2 MB of free disk space

SnapBack DatArrest

DatArrest is a tool used for disk imaging and file recovery. A user can make an image of a server while it is running and being used. When using DatArrest, a user can copy the following:

- Server or PC hard drive to removable media
- Hard drive to hard drive
- Tape to tape

Images captured by DatArrest contain all the system software, networking software, associated drivers, software applications, configurations, data files, and CMOS settings for the system.

SafeBack

SafeBack is a data acquisition tool that investigators can use to create bitstream backups of entire hard drives or partitions on hard drives. It ensures data integrity using CRC-32. SafeBack creates a log file of all transactions it performs.

Data Acquisition Hardware Tools

Forensic investigators use a variety of hardware tools to acquire data from a suspect's computer systems both in the lab and in the field. Some of these tools acquire data by connecting directly to the storage devices, while others can acquire data through Firewire or USB ports.

Image MASSter Solo-3

The Image MASSter Solo-3 is a lightweight handheld tool that investigators use to acquire data. It can pull data off of PATA, SATA, and SCSI notebook and desktop hard drives. It can also pull data off of flash memory cards. An investigator can also connect the device to a computer's USB or Firewire port and acquire data from any storage device in the system. The Image MASSter Solo-3 can copy up to two evidence disks at a time at speeds exceeding 3 GB/min.

The following are the specifications of the Image MASSter Solo-3:

- *Supply voltage*: 90–230 V/50–60 Hz
- *Power consumption*: 10 W without drives
- *Operating temperature*: 5°C–55°C
- *Relative humidity*: 20 percent to 60 percent noncondensing
- *Net weight*: 2.2 lbs
- *Overall dimensions*: 8.3″ × 5.8″ × 2.2″
- *Power supply*: UL and PSU certified, with universal autoswitching input voltage

The following are some of the features of the Image MASSter Solo-3:

- *MD5 and CRC-32 hashing*: MD5 and CRC-32 hashing ensure data integrity.

- *Touch-screen user interface*: The unit's advanced touch-screen user interface and programmable keyboard provide for ease of use.

- *Built-in write protection*: The suspect drive's data is protected with built-in write protection.

- *Audit trail and logs*: An investigator can print detailed operational event log information or save it to a CompactFlash card.

- *Upgradeability*: An investigator can perform software and firmware upgrades using a CompactFlash card.

The following are some of the software features of the Image MASSter Solo-3:

- *Device configuration overlay (DCO) option*: DCO can be used to hide and protect part of a drive from the operating system and file system. If the Image MASSter Solo-3 detects a DCO on a suspect's drive, it can capture this hidden data.

- *Host protected area (HPA) option*: An HPA may exist on a drive, hiding a certain portion of the drive's contents from the operating system and file system. If an HPA exists on a suspect's drive, the ImageMASSter Solo-3 can acquire data stored in the HPA.

- *WipeOut DoD option*: WipeOut was designed to meet the U.S. Department of Defense specification DOD 5220-22M, regarding the sanitization of hard disk drive data. WipeOut performs three iterations to completely erase the contents of a hard drive.

- *WipeOut fast option*: The WipeOut fast option provides a quick non-DoD method of sanitizing a drive of all previously stored data.

- *Linux dd capture option*: The Linux dd capture option captures data as individual Linux dd segmented files. This option allows an investigator to perform multiple data acquisition operations using the same evidence drive.

LinkMASSter-2

The LinkMASSter-2 acquires data from a laptop or desktop by imaging a suspect's hard drive through the computer's USB or Firewire ports. It captures data at speeds exceeding 3 GB/min. It uses write protection and supports MD5, CRC-32, and SHA-1 hashing to ensure data integrity.

The following are the specifications of the LinkMASSter-2:

- *Supply voltage*: 100–240 V/50–60 Hz
- *Power consumption*: 3.5 W without drives
- *Operating temperature*: 5°C–55°C
- *Relative humidity*: 20 percent to 60 percent noncondensing
- *Net weight*: 0.55 lb

- *Overall dimensions*: 5.5″ × 3″ × 1″
- *Power supply*: universal autoswitching input voltage

The following are some of the features of the LinkMASSter-2:

- *Forensic toolkit graphical user interface*: The LinkMASSter-2 forensic toolkit application provides all the tools necessary to perform high-speed data acquisition operations. The interface runs on the Windows XP Professional platform.
- *Multiple media support*: The device supports data transfers between PATA, SATA, and SCSI hard drives. With its built-in 2.5″ interface, it supports capturing data to notebook drives.
- *Audit trail and logs*: An investigator can print detailed operational event log information or save it.

The following are some of the software features of the LinkMASSter-2:

- *LinkMASSter application*: The LinkMASSter application is run from the supplied LinkMASSter bootable CD, which provides write protection for the suspect's drive during initialization and during data acquisition.
- *Single capture option*: The single capture option allows an investigator to acquire data using a forensic sector-by-sector format method.
- *Linux dd capture option*: The Linux dd capture option supports seizing the entire contents of a suspect's drive by capturing data as individual Linux dd segmented files, which are then stored in individual subdirectories on the evidence drive. This option allows any number of seizures to be performed using the same evidence drive, provided there is adequate space to save the seized data.
- *Intelligent capture option*: The intelligent capture option (IQCopy) provides a fast method of acquiring data from FAT16, FAT32, and NTFS. This method analyzes the file system and captures only the allocated drive space.
- *WipeOut DoD option*: This option is designed to erase all data on disk drives. WipeOut was designed to meet the U.S. Department of Defense specification DOD 5220-22M, regarding the sanitization of hard disk drives.
- *WipeOut fast option*: The WipeOut fast option provides a quick non-DoD method of sanitizing a drive of all previously stored data.

RoadMASSter-2

The RoadMASSter-2 is a forensic data acquisition and analysis tool designed for use in the field. It provides an investigator with all the tools necessary to acquire and analyze data from Firewire and USB ports, flash memory cards, and PATA, SATA, and SCSI disks.

The following are the specifications of the RoadMASSter-2:

- *Supply voltage*: 100–240 V/50–60 Hz
- *Power consumption*: 150 W without drives

- *Operating temperature*: 5°C–55°C
- *Relative humidity*: 20 percent to 60 percent noncondensing
- *Net weight*: 32 lbs
- *Overall dimensions*: 13″ × 21″ × 7.5″
- *Power supply*: universal autoswitching input voltage
- *Processor*: AMD64 3500+
- *Memory*: 2 GB RAM
- *Hard drive*: 60 GB 7200 rpm internal IDE drive
- *Other storage*: CD-RW, DVD+RW, DVD-RW, floppy disk
- *Display*: 15″ TFT color LCD display
- *Card reader/writer*: 1–7 multicard read/write slots and 1–7 multicard read-only slots
- *Sound system*: Stereo speakers and line in/line out connector
- *Operating system*: Windows XP Professional

The following are some of the features of the RoadMASSter-2:

- *MD5, CRC-32, and SHA-1 hashing*: These hashing techniques ensure data integrity.
- *Forensic toolkit graphical user interface*: The RoadMASSter-2 forensic toolkit application provides an investigator with all the tools necessary to perform high-speed forensic data acquisition operations.
- *High-speed operation*: Data transfer rates can exceed 3.3 GB/min.
- *Multiple capture methods*: Investigators can acquire data using a forensic sector-by-sector format method or using a Linux dd segmented file format method. The Linux dd capture method allows an investigator to put multiple images on one evidence drive.
- *Built-in write protection*: The data on the suspect's drive is protected with built-in write protection.
- *Multiple media support*: The RoadMASSter-2 supports data transfers between PATA, SATA, and SCSI hard disk drives. Interface ports and readers are available to support flash memory cards, external Firewire and USB drives, and DVD and CD media. The built-in 2.5″ interface supports notebook drives.
- *Preview and analysis*: The toolkit provides an investigator with the capability to preview and analyze a suspect's write-protected data.
- *Audit trail and logs*: An investigator can print detailed operational event log information or save it.

The following are some of the software features of the RoadMASSter-2:

- *WipeOut DoD option*: This option is designed to completely erase data on disk drives. WipeOut was designed to meet the U.S. Department of Defense specification DOD 5220-22M, regarding the sanitization of hard disk drives.

- *WipeOut fast option*: The WipeOut fast option provides an investigator with a quick non-DoD method of sanitizing a drive.

- *LinkMASSter application*: The LinkMASSter application is run from the supplied LinkMASSter bootable CD, which provides write protection for the suspect's drive during initialization and during data acquisition.

- *Intelligent capture mode*: The intelligent capture option (IQCopy) provides a fast method of acquiring data from FAT16, FAT32, and NTFS. This method analyzes the file system and captures only the allocated drive space.

Data Duplication Software Tools

Computer forensic investigators have many software tools at their disposal for the purpose of data duplication. These tools provide high-speed backup and imaging capabilities.

R-Drive Image

R-Drive Image is a software tool used to create disk images with various compression levels for backup or duplication purposes. A disk image file contains an exact byte-by-byte copy of a hard drive, partition, or logical disk. These image files can then be stored on a variety of media, including removable media such as CD-RWs and DVD-RWs.

DriveLook

DriveLook provides access to remote drives through serial cables or TCP/IP.

Forensic investigators use this tool to:

- Index a drive for all text that has ever been written to it
- Search the drive for particular words
- View the location of words in a disk editor
- Switch between hex and text views
- Use image files as input

DiskExplorer

The DiskExplorer tool is a sophisticated disk editor that allows a forensic investigator to investigate a FAT or NTFS drive and recover data from it. Figure 2-3 shows a screen displaying the partition table of a drive.

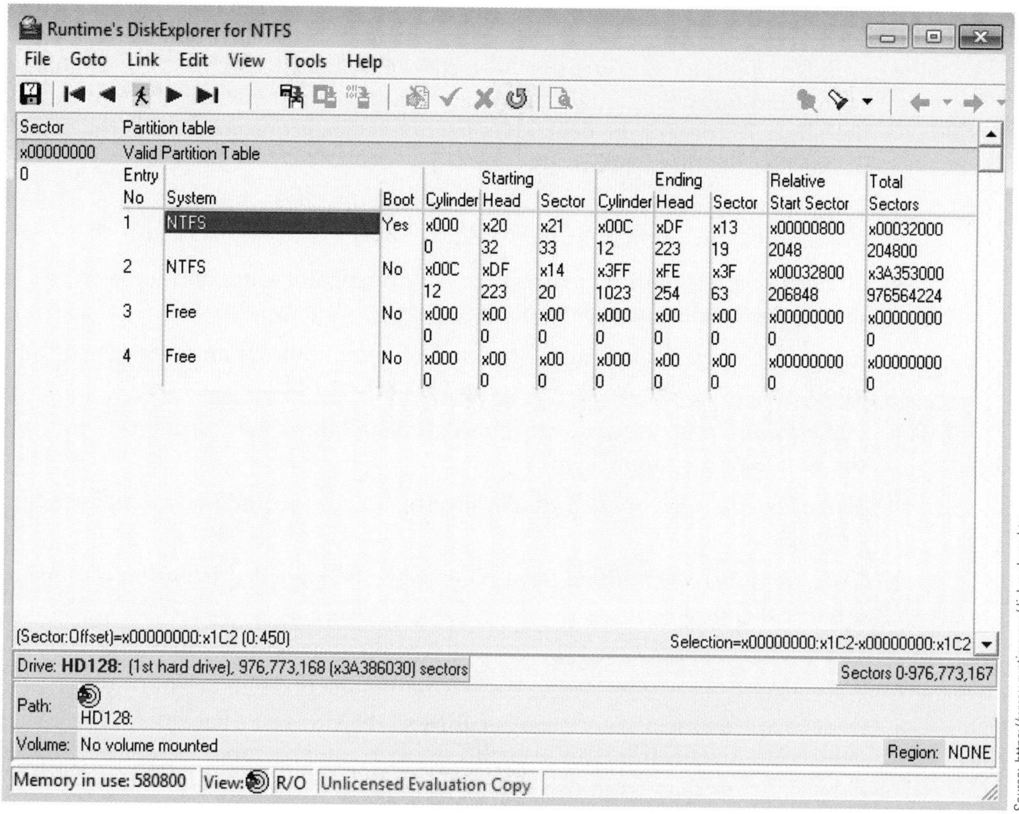

Source: https://www.runtime.org/diskexplorer.htm

Figure 2-3 DiskExplorer allows an investigator to recover data.

An investigator can perform the following tasks using DiskExplorer:

- Navigate through the drive by jumping to the partition table, boot record, master file table, and root directory
- Choose between views such as hex, text, index allocation, MFT, boot record, and partition table, and inspect file entry details
- Save files and directories from anywhere on the drive
- Identify the file a certain cluster belongs to
- Create a virtual volume when the boot record is lost or corrupt
- Edit the disk drive by using the direct read/write mode or the virtual write mode

Save-N-Sync

Save-N-Sync allows an investigator to synchronize and back up files from a source folder on one computer to a target folder on a second networked computer or local storage device. An investigator can manually or automatically schedule regular synchronization and backup operations. It works on Windows NT/2000/XP/2003/Vista/7/8.

The following are some of the features of Save-N-Sync:

- *Standard and bidirectional synchronization*: Standard synchronization compares source and target files, and new or updated files on the source PC are copied to the target PC or storage device. Bidirectional synchronization adds the extra step of copying the files back to the source.
- *Daily timer*: This feature allows an investigator to schedule file synchronizations for any time on any day of the week.
- *Unobtrusive background processing*: An investigator can continue working, even during the synchronization process.
- *Embedded open file manager option*: This option allows an investigator to back up locked files, such as Outlook and QuickBooks files.
- *File attribute transfers*: File attributes are maintained when a file is copied from the source to the target.
- *Extensive filtering capabilities*: An investigator can include or exclude specific files or folders.
- *Command-line capabilities*: Save-N-Sync can be launched from the command line, a batch file, or a script.

DFSMSdss

Data set services (dss) is a component of IBM's DFSMS (Data Facility Storage Management Subsystem). An investigator can use this tool to quickly and efficiently duplicate data. DFSMSdss can copy data from one disk to another or from a disk to a tape.

The following are some of the features of DFSMSdss:

- *Movement and replication of data*: The tool offers powerful, user-friendly functions that allow an investigator to move or copy data between volumes of like and unlike device types. It can also copy data that has been backed up.
- *Backup and recovery of data*: With this tool, an investigator can back up and recover data at both the data set and volume levels. An investigator can also use DFSMSdss to restore vital system packs during disaster recovery without a host operating system.
- *Conversion of data sets and volumes*: DFSMSdss converts data sets and volumes to system-managed storage, or returns data to a non-system-managed state, as part of a recovery procedure that doesn't include moving data.

SCSIPAK

SCSIPAK is a software-based data conversion and duplication system. SCSIPAK is a set of system tools that extend the support of tape drives under Microsoft Windows NT and Windows 2000.

These tools allow an investigator to identify drives on a SCSI bus, transfer data between disks and tapes or optical discs, and copy data between tapes or optical discs.

SCSIPAK reads data from a tape or optical disc and simultaneously writes it to up to seven drives at once. The image file from the tape or optical medium is stored along with an index file, which contains details of the tape file and set marks, directory partitions, or unused optical sectors. This allows an investigator to duplicate even complex-format tapes and optical discs.

Data Duplication Hardware Tools

The data duplication hardware tools that forensic investigators use are high-speed, high-volume devices. Most of these tools also provide investigators with the capability to completely erase data from a disk.

The Image MASSter 4000PRO X2 SAS

The Image MASSter 4000PRO X2 SAS has double the power of its original version and features native support for SAS, SATA, and USB 3.0 drives in addition to other common drive interfaces through the use of optional adapters. Its units come with built-in support to connect an optional Eight Drive add-on module, providing the capability to copy and wipe up to 16 drives at the same time. This tool supports SHA-1 and SHA-2 hardware accelerated drive hashing as well as the standard MD-5 hashing method. Utilizing the NIST-approved AES-256 encryption standard, the built-in hard drive encryption support can secure a target drive's data. Units feature a 1 GB ethernet connection to upload or download drive images to a network storage area. It also has an internal PCIe expansion slot which can be used to expand the unit's capability to support additional drive interfaces such as SCSI and FireWire. Users can add 10 GB Ethernet connectivity if needed. (Source: Copyright 2015 **ICS**. All Rights Reserved.)

Disk Jockey IT Pro

Disk Jockey IT Pro is a high-speed data duplication tool. It can copy data from PATA and SATA desktop and laptop drives. It is a lightweight handheld device that can copy data to one or two target drives at speeds exceeding 2 GB/min.

The following are some of the features of the Disk Jockey IT Pro:

- *Stand-alone HD mode*: An investigator can mount one or two PATA or SATA hard drives on a Windows or Macintosh computer, through Firewire or USB 2.0, without installing any extra drivers. The Disk Jockey IT Pro includes 2.5″ laptop adapter cables and 3.5″ desktop cables.

- *Mirroring*: The Disk Jockey IT Pro allows an investigator to mirror two hard drives for real-time backup (RAID 1). If one drive fails, there will be no downtime, as the data is stored simultaneously on the second drive.

- *Spanning*: An investigator can easily make one large logical volume from two disks attached to the Disk Jockey IT Pro. The investigator can then connect the Disk Jockey IT Pro to a Firewire or USB port on a Windows or Macintosh computer to access the two drives as standard external storage.

- *Disk copy compare/verification*: This feature allows an investigator to verify that a copy is an exact duplicate, ensuring that there is no data loss.

- *Hard disk read test*: The Disk Jockey IT Pro can perform a sector-by-sector hard disk read test to test the overall health of a hard drive.

- *Two levels of erasure*: The Disk Jockey IT Pro offers two levels of disk erasure. The first is a fast, one-pass erase. The second is a more thorough three-pass erase that an investigator can use when he or she needs to feel more confident that the data is irretrievably erased.

QuickCopy

QuickCopy is a tape duplication system. The following are some of the features of QuickCopy:

- Duplicates a master tape to one or more target tapes
- Duplicates from master images stored on local or network hard drives
- Capable of multitasking for mixed jobs. For instance, it can duplicate a 4-mm tape and a DLT simultaneously.
- Provides 100 percent verification of all copies made
- Uses the Microsoft NT operating system and graphical user interface (GUI)
- Can also copy CD media with the QuickCopy-CD option

Chapter Summary

- This chapter has discussed the different procedures that forensic investigators follow in the duplication, acquisition, and preservation of data.

- Investigators can acquire data in three ways: by creating a bitstream disk-to-image file, by making a bitstream disk-to-disk copy, or by creating a sparse data copy of a specific folder or file.

- Data duplication is essential for the proper preservation of digital evidence.

- Windows data acquisition tools allow an investigator to easily acquire evidence from a disk with the help of removable media, such as USB storage devices.

- Forensic investigators use the built-in Linux command dd to copy data from a disk drive.

- The SavePart command generates an image of a partition on a hard disk.

Key Terms

data acquisition	sparse data copy	User Datagram Protocol (UDP)
data duplication	Transmission Control Protocol (TCP)	

Review Questions

1. What are the methods investigators use to acquire digital evidence?

_____

_____

_____

_____

2. What do the SavePart and WritePart commands in DriveSpy do?

_____

_____

_____

_____

3. Why is there a need for data duplication?

_____

_____

_____

_____

4. How is netcat used with dd to acquire data?

_____

_____

_____

_____

5. Write down the hardware tools used for data acquisition.

_____

_____

_____

_____

6. Write down the hardware tools used for data duplication.

_____

_____

_____

_____

7. What file systems does dd work with?

_____

_____

_____

_____

8. Describe the features of QuickCopy.

_____

_____

_____

_____

9. What are the system requirements for Drive SnapShot?

_____

_____

_____

_____

Hands-On Projects

1. Download an EnCase image file:
   - Using your preferred Internet browser, navigate to *http://www. forensickb.com/2008/01/forensic-practical-2.html* and download the image file in EnCase format. The filename will be "WinXP.E01" (Figure 2-4).

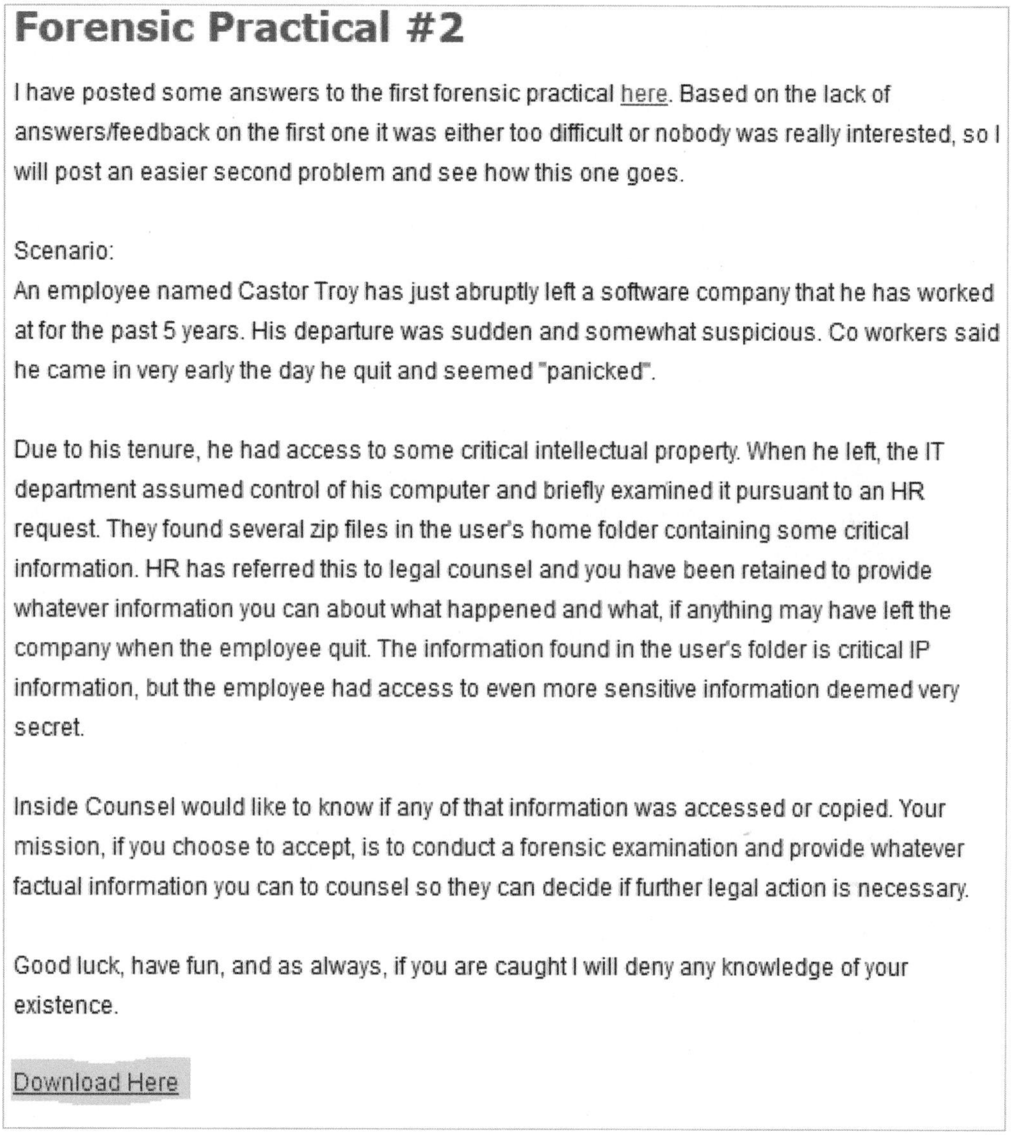

Forensic Practical #2

I have posted some answers to the first forensic practical here. Based on the lack of answers/feedback on the first one it was either too difficult or nobody was really interested, so I will post an easier second problem and see how this one goes.

Scenario:

An employee named Castor Troy has just abruptly left a software company that he has worked at for the past 5 years. His departure was sudden and somewhat suspicious. Co workers said he came in very early the day he quit and seemed "panicked".

Due to his tenure, he had access to some critical intellectual property. When he left, the IT department assumed control of his computer and briefly examined it pursuant to an HR request. They found several zip files in the user's home folder containing some critical information. HR has referred this to legal counsel and you have been retained to provide whatever information you can about what happened and what, if anything may have left the company when the employee quit. The information found in the user's folder is critical IP information, but the employee had access to even more sensitive information deemed very secret.

Inside Counsel would like to know if any of that information was accessed or copied. Your mission, if you choose to accept, is to conduct a forensic examination and provide whatever factual information you can to counsel so they can decide if further legal action is necessary.

Good luck, have fun, and as always, if you are caught I will deny any knowledge of your existence.

Download Here

Source: EnCase

Figure 2-4 Download link for EnCase image file "WinXP.E01".

- Save this image for use in the next project.
- Read the scenario and comments section and begin to formulate a plan of attack on how you would analyze this image.
- Prepare a one-paragraph summary detailing specific things you would look for in this image and which previously used tools may assist you in your efforts.

2. Use Mount Image Pro to mount an EnCase image file:
   - Using your preferred Internet browser, navigate to *http://www.mountimage.com/* to download Mount Image Pro.
   - Click the link "**Current Version: v6.1.3.1626**" to download Mount Image Pro.
   - Click the link to "**Request a 30-day evaluation key**" (Figure 2-5).

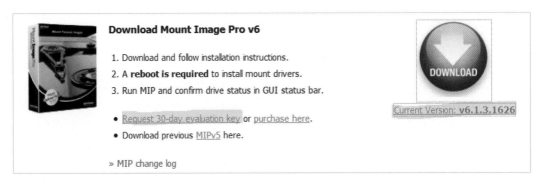

Figure 2-5   Download links for "Mount Image Pro" and "30-day evaluation key".

- Install Mount Image Pro.
- Launch Mount Image Pro, choose "**Online Activation**" and enter the license key received via email.
- Click "**Mount**", click "**Add Image**", locate the WinXP.E01 image file downloaded in Hands-on Project 1 and click "**Open**".
- Select the "**WinXP.E01**" image file and click "**Mount**".

- Set the "**Mount As**" selection to "**Disk**".
- Set the "**Access Mode**" selection to "**Read Only**".
- Click "**OK**" (Figure 2-6).

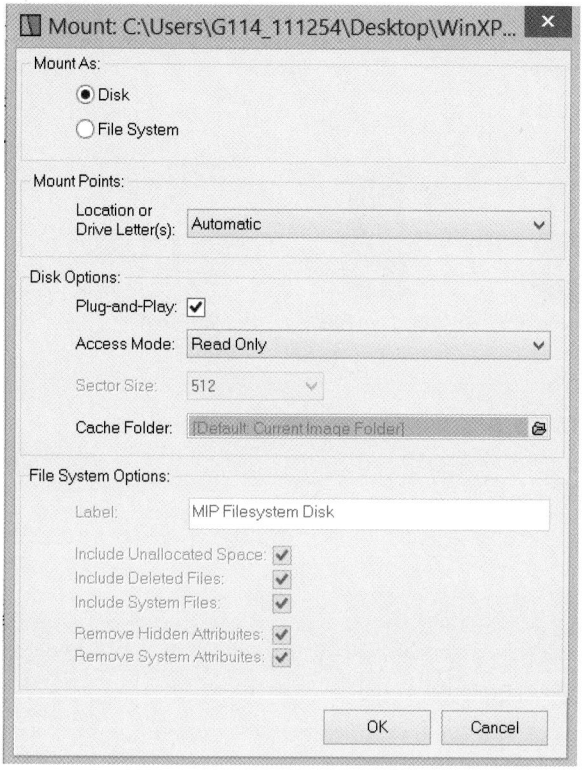

Source: Mount Image Pro

Figure 2-6 Mount options dialog window.

- The mounted image will be assigned an available drive letter and will open in Windows Explorer (Figure 2-7).

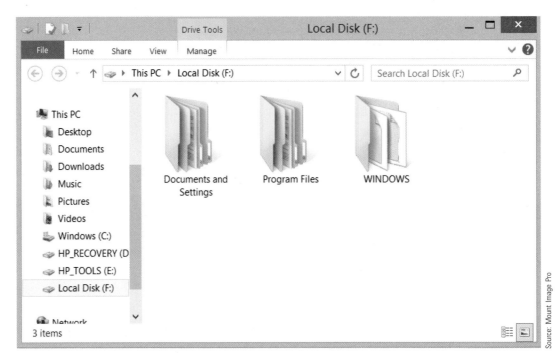

Figure 2-7   Mounted image in Windows Explorer.

- Select the mounted image in Mount Image Pro to view the properties of the image file (Figure 2-8).

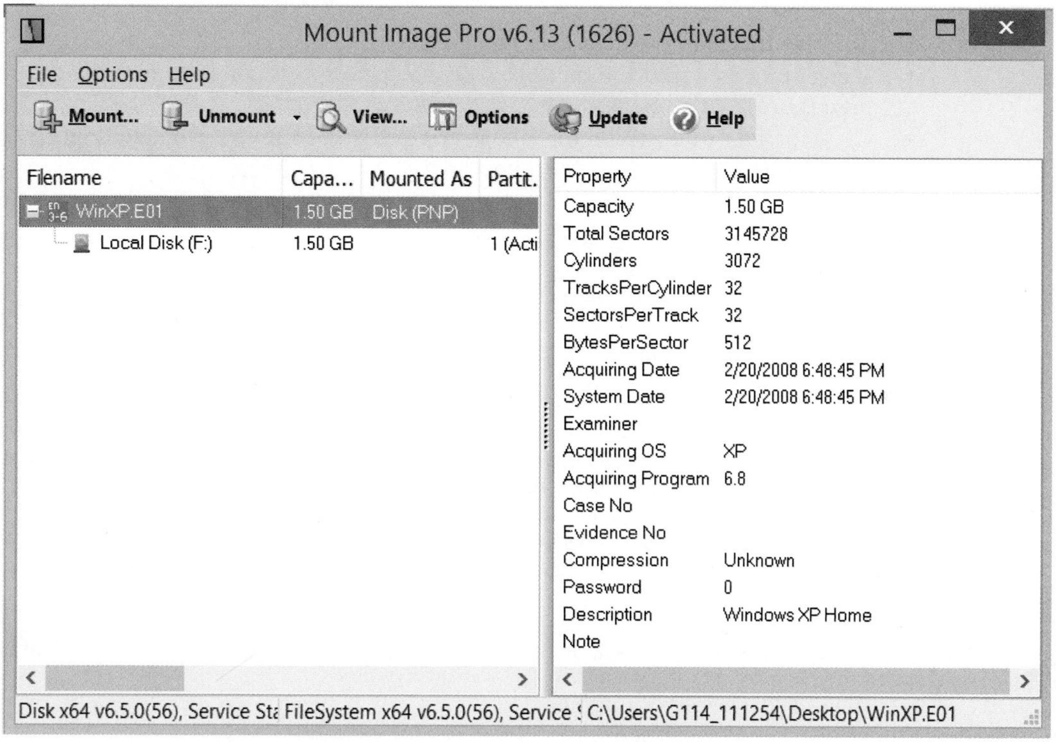

Source: Mount Image Pro

Figure 2-8 Mount Image Pro properties of mounted image "WinXP.E01".

- Explore the contents of the mounted image file, then perform 2-3 of the forensic tasks you identified in Hands-on Project 1.
- Prepare a one-paragraph summary detailing your efforts and any potential evidence obtained in reference to the scenario.

3. Use R-Drive Image to create a disk image:
   - Using your preferred Internet browser, navigate to *http://www.drive-image.com/* to download R-Drive Image.
   - Click the link to download a 30-day trial version of R-Drive Image (Figure 2-9).

R-Drive Image restores the images on the original disks, on any other partitions or even on a hard drive's free space on the fly. To restore system and other locked partitions R-Drive Image is switched to the pseudo-graphic mode directly from Windows or bootable version created by the utility is launched from CD disc or diskettes.

Using R-Drive Image, you can completely and rapidly restore your system after heavy data loss caused by an operating system crash, virus attack or hardware failure. You can also use R-Drive Image for mass system deployment when you need to setup many identical computers. In other words, you can manually setup one system only, create an image of the system, and then deploy it on all other computers, saving your time and costs. If you need to restore only certain files from a disk image, you can connect that image as a virtual disk and copy those files directly from the disk image using Windows Explorer or any other file utility.

R-Drive Image is one of the best backup and disaster recovery solutions to prevent losing your data after a fatal system failure.

A free fully functional 30-day trial version is available for evaluation purpose.

Source: R-Drive Image

Figure 2-9   Download link for "R-Drive Image".

- Install R-Drive Image.
- Launch R-Drive Image and click "**Next**" to accept the 30-day trial.
- Select "**Create an Image**" and then click "**Next**" (Figure 2-10).

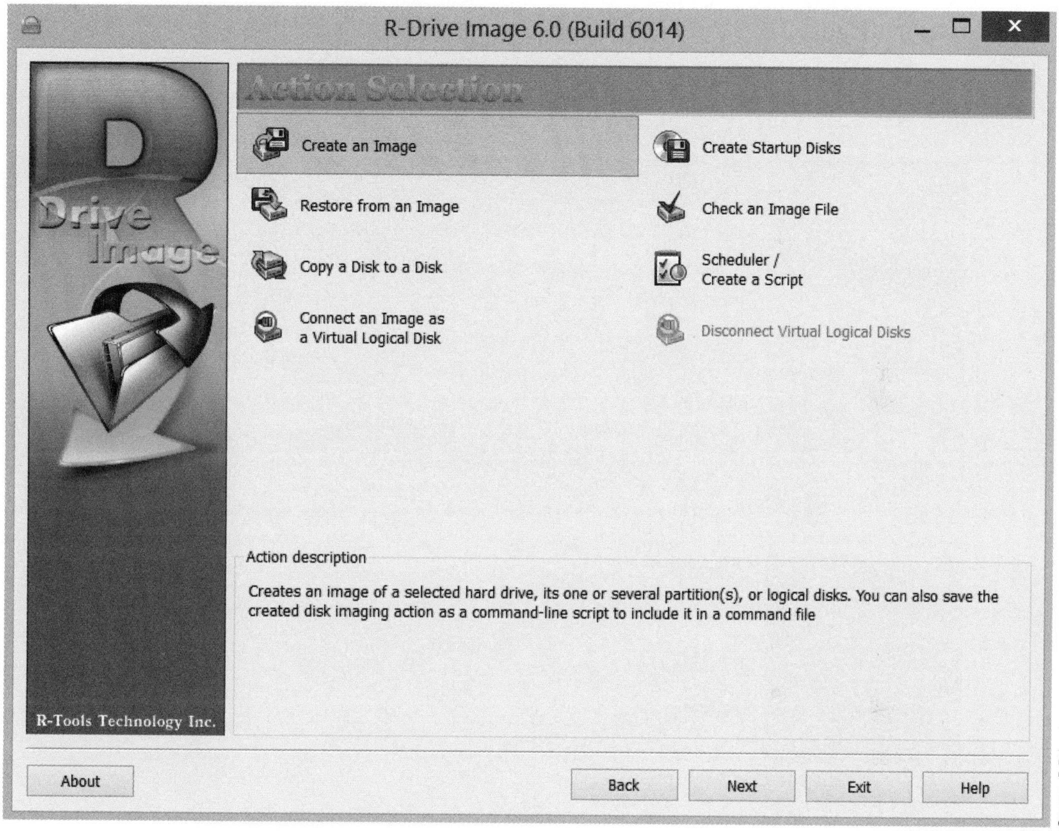

Source: R-Drive Image

Figure 2-10 R-Drive Image "Action Selection" window.

- Select a partition from your system to create an image of and then click "**Next**".
- Select a destination for the image file and then click "**Next**".
- At the next screen, examine the parameters to determine if the destination you selected is large enough to accommodate the image. Explore the other available options and then click "**Exit**". You will not actually create an image in this project (Figure 2-11).

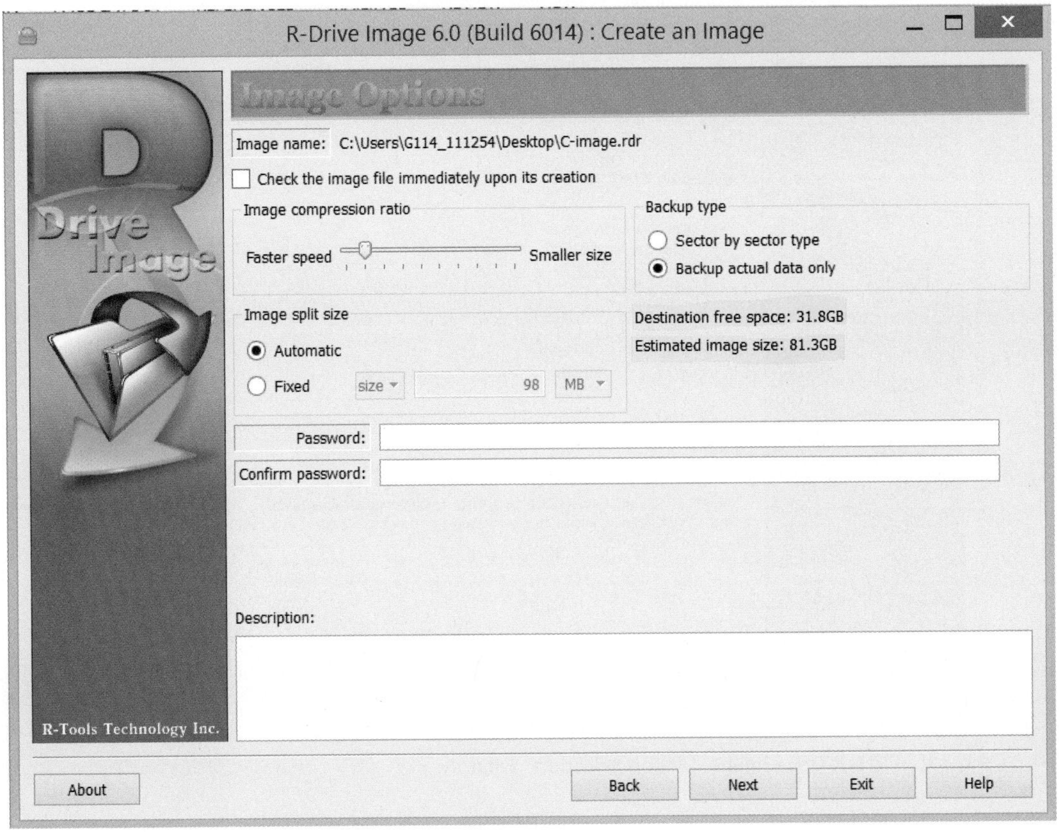

Source: R-Drive Image

Figure 2-11 R-Drive Image "Image Options" window.

- Prepare a one-paragraph summary explaining the potential uses for R-Drive Image in a forensic investigation.

chapter 3

Forensic Investigations Using EnCase

After completing this chapter, you should be able to:

- Understand evidence files
- Verify evidence file integrity
- Perform hashing
- Configure EnCase
- Search using EnCase
- Use bookmarks in EnCase
- View recovered files
- Understand the master boot record
- Understand the NTFS starting point
- Understand hash values
- Perform signature analysis
- Perform e-mail recovery

What If?

In Chapter 1, you read a case about Jeremy Johnson, a former teacher in the Adams Central School District. Johnson was arrested and jailed on 19 charges of child seduction, a Class D felony. Assuming the case in Chapter 1 is still active, answer the following questions:

- How could investigators have used EnCase to gather evidence?
- How could these investigators prove the integrity of the evidence gathered?

Introduction to Forensic Investigation Using EnCase

This chapter focuses on forensic investigation using EnCase. EnCase is a forensic software suite that provides investigators with a full set of tools for forensic investigations. The chapter gives some information about EnCase and discusses how investigators can use EnCase to perform different forensic tasks.

Evidence Files

An evidence file is the core component of EnCase. It is a proprietary file created by EnCase to compress and preserve bitstream images of acquired media. The EnCase evidence file is widely known throughout the law enforcement and computer security industries. Courts in the United States, including at the federal appellate level, and in the international community have accepted EnCase evidence files in both civil and criminal cases.

EnCase evidence files are used to preserve evidence and continue the examination without having to restore the image to separate media. The bitstream image in an EnCase evidence file can be mounted as a read-only file or virtual drive, from which EnCase reconstructs the file structure using the logical data in the bitstream image. This allows the investigator to search and examine the contents of the acquired drive within the EnCase Enterprise Examiner environment. The EnCase evidence file contains an exact copy of the data from the original media, including time stamps, deleted files, unallocated space, and file-system attributes. An investigator can easily transfer an EnCase evidence file to different types of media and archive it for future reference. If necessary, an investigator can also use the evidence file to restore the exact image to another hard drive. An evidence file consists of the following:

- *Header*: The header contains the date and time of evidence acquisition, the examiner's name, notes on the acquisition, an optional password, and its own **cyclic redundancy check** (CRC) checksum. **CRC** is a type of function that takes a quantity of data of any size and produces an output of a fixed length, usually a 32-bit integer that is generally used to verify the integrity of the original data. A **checksum** is a fixed-size integer resulting from the application of this algorithm. The header is always prefixed with *Case Info*.

- *Checksum*: One of the main parts of an EnCase evidence file is CRC checksums. An evidence file saves checksums for every block of 64 sectors (~32 KB) of evidence.

- *Data blocks*: Data blocks contain an exact replica of the original evidence. EnCase saves a bitstream image of evidence.

- *Footer*: The footer contains an MD5 hash for the entire bitstream image.

Verifying Evidence Files

After burning the discs, an investigator can run **Verify Evidence Files** from the **Tools** menu on each disc to verify that the burn was thorough and that the evidence file segment is intact.

Evidence File Format

Each evidence file is an exact sector-by-sector copy of a floppy or hard disk. Every byte of the file is verified using a 32-bit CRC, and it is virtually impossible to tamper with the evidence once it has been acquired.

EnCase uses ASR Data's Expert Witness Compression Format for storing images of evidence; this format can reduce file sizes by up to 50 percent.

EnCase can store media data in multiple evidence files called segment files. Each segment file consists of multiple sections. Each section consists of a section start definition. This definition contains a section type.

From version 4 onward, EnCase has had two header sections, header and header2. The header section is defined once, and the header2 section is defined twice within the file; both copies of header2 contain the same information.

Verifying File Integrity

Whenever an investigator adds an evidence file to a case, he or she can use EnCase to verify the integrity of the file.

Hashing

Hashing is a well-defined mathematical function that converts a large variable-sized amount of data into a small fixed-length integer that may serve as an index into an array, as a method obscuring and protecting passwords being transferred over a network, or to verify the integrity of stored data. EnCase calculates an MD5 hash when it acquires a physical drive or logical drive, as shown in Figure 3-1.

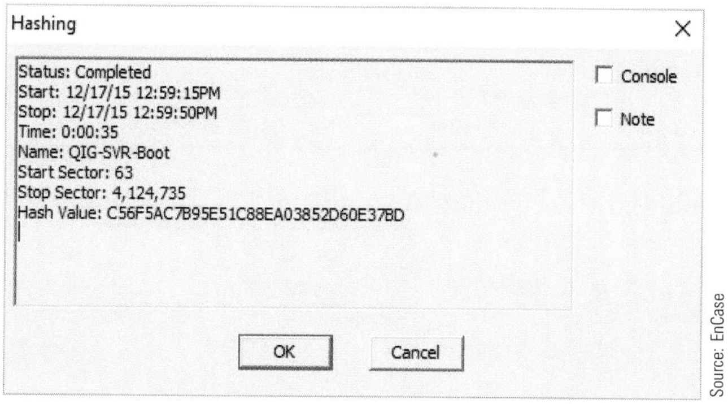

Figure 3-1   MD5 hashing helps to verify file integrity.

Acquiring an Image

An investigator can acquire an image by performing the following steps:

1. Click **File** and then **Add Device** to acquire the image. The investigator can alternately click the **Add Device** button on the toolbar. Figure 3-2 shows a screenshot of this process.

2. Select the device type. If the device is a USB drive, it should not be connected to the forensic computer prior to the boot process.

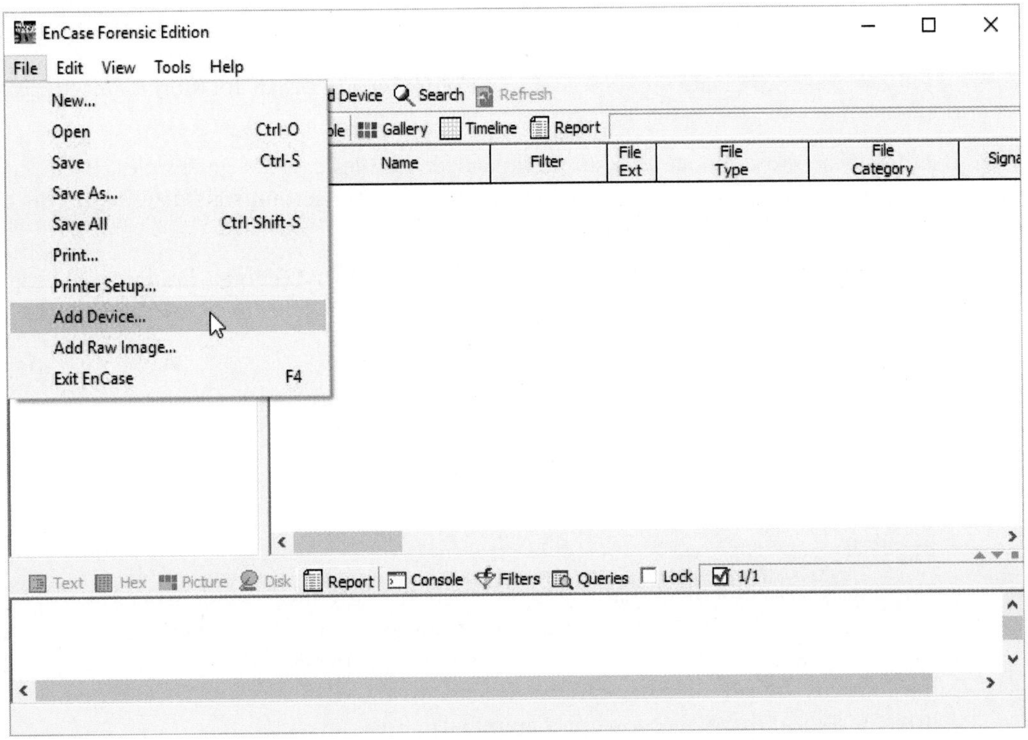

Figure 3-2   An investigator can acquire an image of a device by adding the device to the evidence file.

Configuring EnCase

An investigator can click **Tools** and then **Options** to configure EnCase. Figures 3-3 and 3-4 depict some of the **Options** screens.

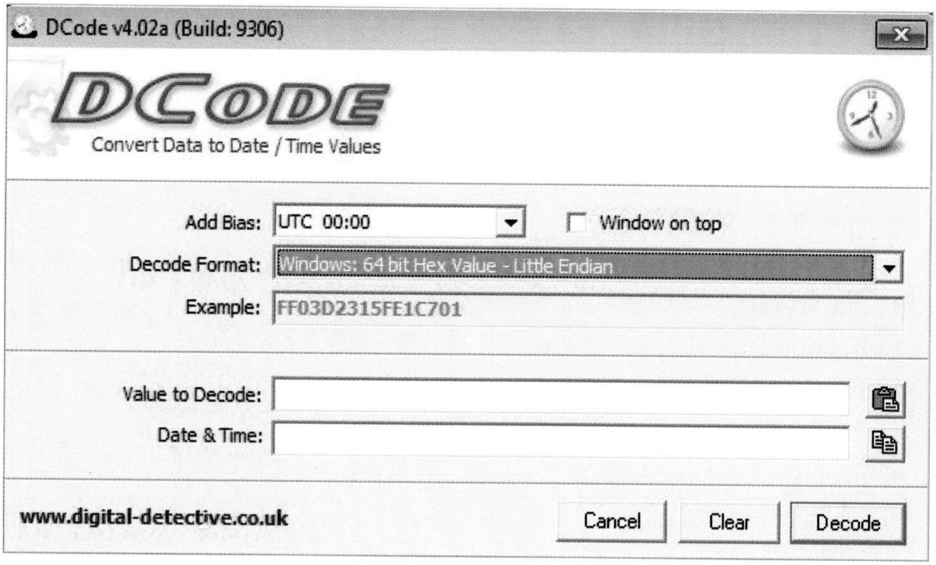

Source: http://www.digital-detective.net

Figure 3-3 The **Case Options** tab allows an investigator to configure basic options about a case.

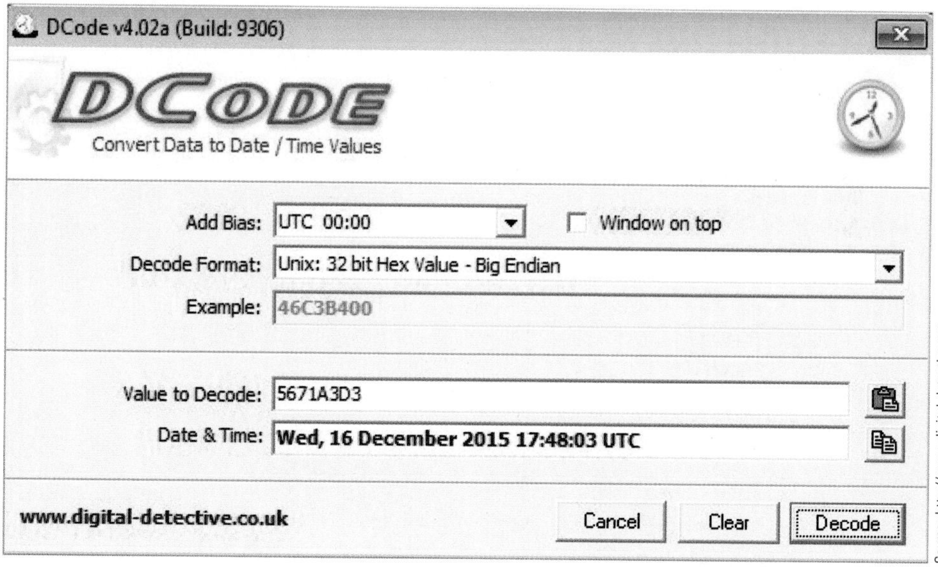

Source: http://www.digital-detective.net

Figure 3-4 The **Global** tab allows an investigator to configure program options.

View Menu

An investigator can launch various utilities using the **View** menu (Figure 3-5). The **View** menu includes the following options:

- Cases
- File types
- File signatures
- File viewers
- Keywords
- Search IDs
- Text styles
- Scripts
- Hash sets
- Encryption keys
- EnScript types

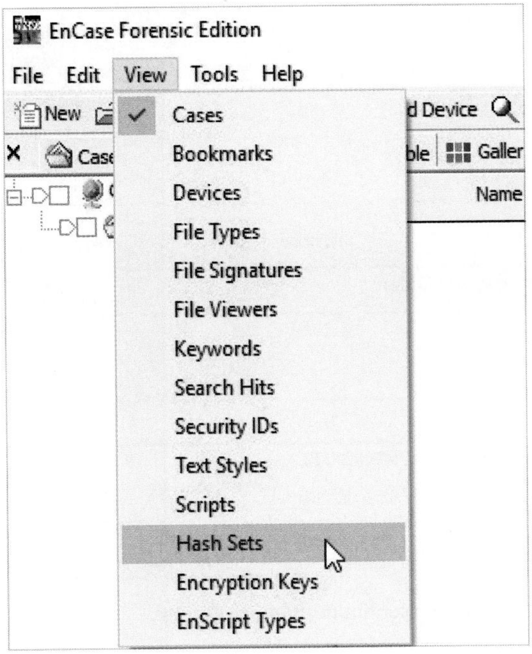

Source: EnCase

Figure 3-5 The **View** menu provides an investigator with many different utilities.

Device Tab

The **Device** report shows information about the currently selected device, as shown in Figure 3-6. The information displayed includes the following:

- Evidence number
- File path
- Examiner name
- Actual date
- Target date
- Total size
- Total sectors
- File integrity
- EnCase version
- System version
- Acquisition hash
- Verify hash
- Notes

Device

Evidence Number:	Item 003
File Path:	E:\Encase_Evidence_E01_Files\Encase Evidence E01 Files\QIG-SVR-Boot2.E01
Examiner Name:	John P Colbert
Actual Date:	07/10/01 03:23:55PM
Target Date:	07/10/01 03:24:46PM
Total Size:	2,111,864,832 bytes (2.0GB)
Total Sectors:	4,124,736
File Integrity:	Completely Verified, 0 Errors
Write Blocker:	FastBloc
EnCase Version:	3.10b
System Version:	Windows 98
Acquisition Hash:	4781C2066348A01F5ED70BA670123340
Verify Hash:	4781C2066348A01F5ED70BA670123340
Notes:	Copyright 2001 Guidance Software, Inc.

Source: EnCase

Figure 3-6   The **Device** report displays important information about an acquired device.

Status Bar

The status bar (Figures 3-7 and 3-8) provides the following sector details for a selected file:

- Physical sector number
- Logical sector number
- Cluster number
- Sector offset

- File offset
- Length

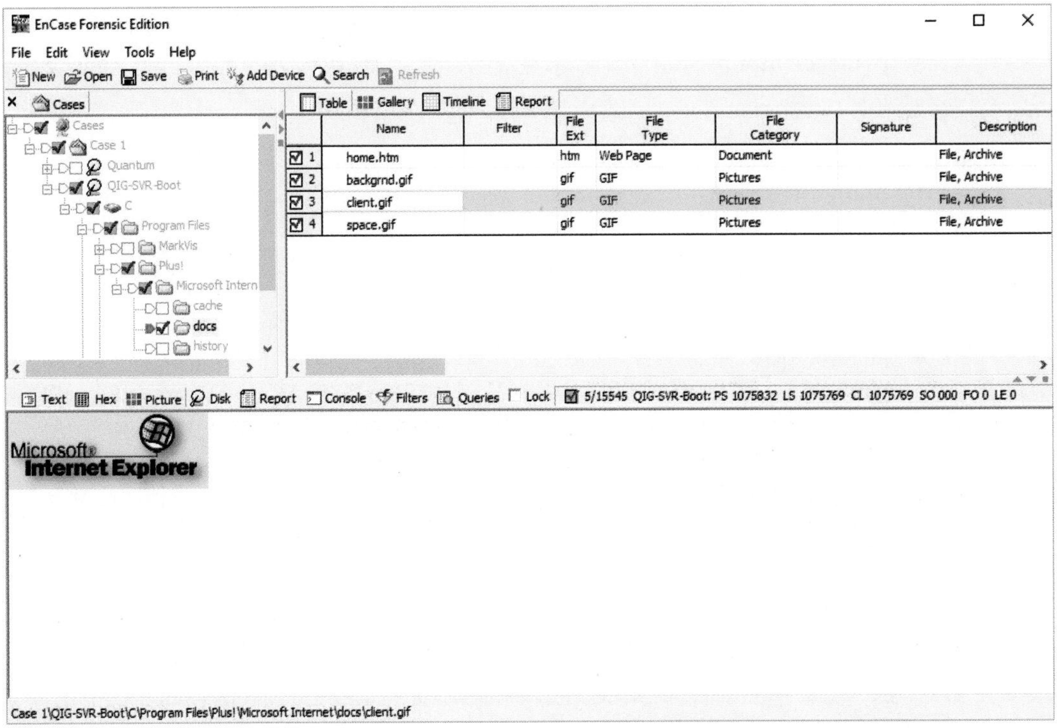

Figure 3-7   An investigator can view information about EnCase's current task in the status bar.

Figure 3-8   A closer view of the status bar.

Source: EnCase

Searching

EnCase provides powerful searching capabilities. An investigator can perform keyword searches at the logical level (file level) or physical level (byte by byte). EnCase can locate information anywhere on physical or logical media by using its deep analysis features. EnCase has the following advanced search capabilities:

- *Concurrent search*
- *Proximity search*
- *Internet and e-mail search*
- *E-mail address search*
- *Global Regular Expressions Post (GREP) search*: The GREP search utility enables the investigator to search for information with a known general format, such as any

telephone numbers, credit card numbers, network IDs, logon records, or IP addresses, even when the specific number is not known.

- *File finder*: This searches within the page file, unallocated clusters, selected files or entire cases, looking for specific file types and structured data.

EnCase provides the following search options:

- *Case sensitive*: EnCase searches for keywords only in the exact case specified in the text box.
- *GREP*: The keyword is a regular expression.
- *RTL reading*: This is a keyword search in a right-to-left sequence for international language support.
- *Active code page*: This option allows an investigator to enter keywords in many different languages.
- *Unicode*: This enables investigators to search for keywords with international language characters.
- *Big-endian Unicode*: This enables investigators to search for keywords with international language characters.

Figure 3-9 shows a screenshot of the **Search** window.

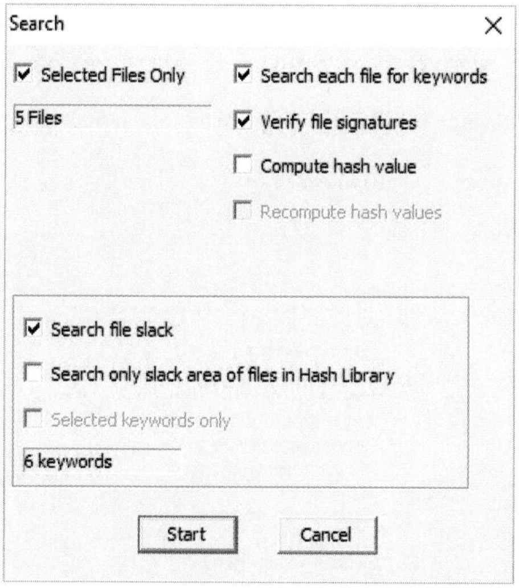

Figure 3-9   The **Search** window allows an investigator to choose different search options.

Keywords

A key component of any search is the keywords and their rules. Keywords are saved in the keywords.ini file. An investigator chooses keywords based on what he or she is investigating. For example, the investigator might want to add keywords such as the following:

- *kill*
- *suicide*
- *cheat*

- *Swiss bank*
- *San Francisco*

Adding Keywords To add keywords, an investigator needs to right-click **Keyword** and select **New**, as shown in Figures 3-10 and 3-11.

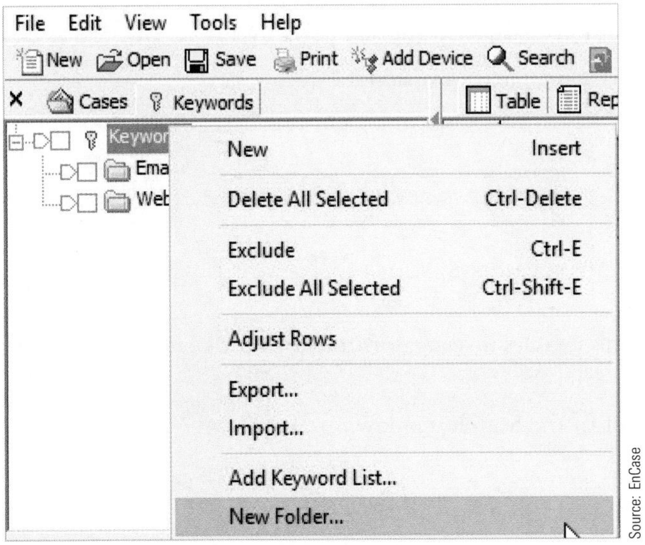

Figure 3-10   The **Keyword** menu allows an investigator to add new keywords to a search.

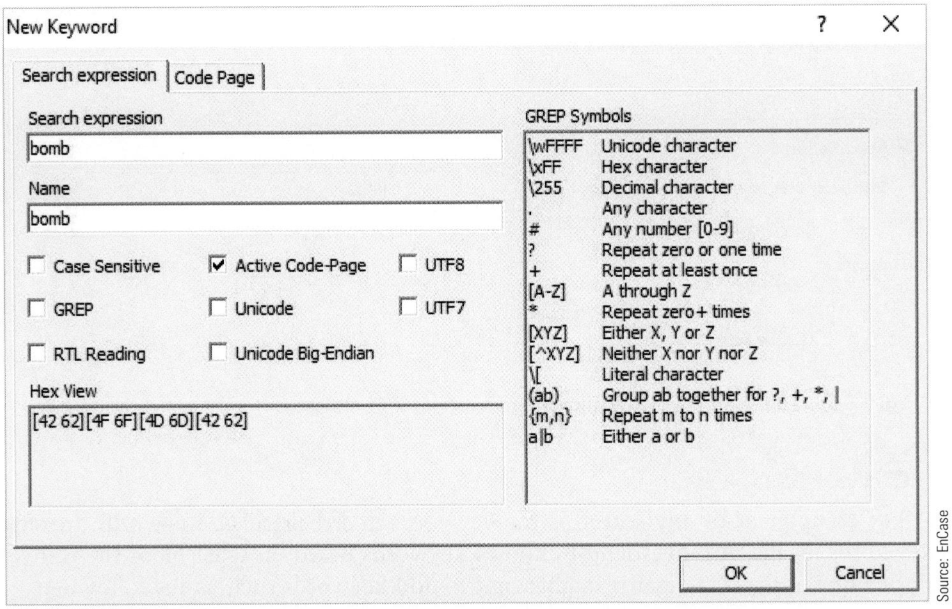

Figure 3-11   An investigator can set options for keywords in the **New Keyword** window.

Grouping Keywords An investigator can group keywords to organize search terms. To do so, he or she right-clicks **Keyword**, selects **New Folder**, and types in a folder name.

Adding Multiple Keywords To add multiple keywords, an investigator can right-click the keyword folder and choose **Add Keyword List**. Figure 3-12 shows a screenshot of the **Add Keyword List** window.

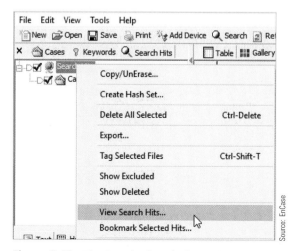

Figure 3-12   The **Add Keyword List** menu allows an investigator to add a list of keywords to a search and set the same options on all of them.

Starting the Search

An investigator can search a set of files, a set of folders, or an entire drive by performing the following steps:

1. Check the keywords that need to be searched.

2. Click the **Search** button.

Search Hits Tab

The **Search Hits** tab reveals the search results, as shown in Figure 3-13.

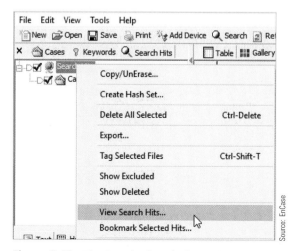

Figure 3-13   The **Search Hits** tab shows the results of a search.

Bookmarks

EnCase allows an investigator to bookmark files, folders, or sections of a file for easy reference. The investigator can view bookmarks by clicking **View** and then **Bookmark**. Figure 3-14 shows the **Bookmarks** tab.

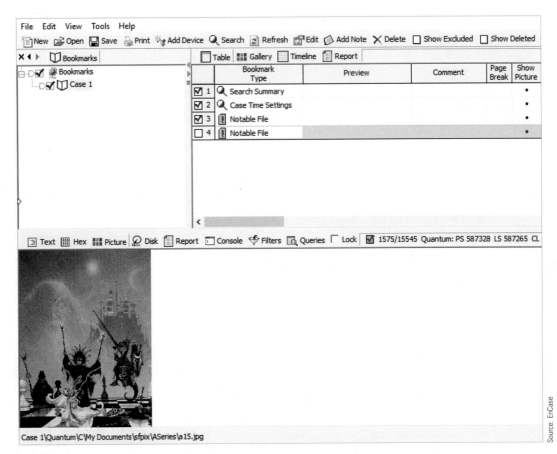

Figure 3-14 The **Bookmarks** tab shows the bookmarks that an investigator has created.

Creating Bookmark Folders

An investigator can create a bookmark folder by checking **Create new bookmark folder** in the **Bookmark Selected Files** window, as shown in Figure 3-15.

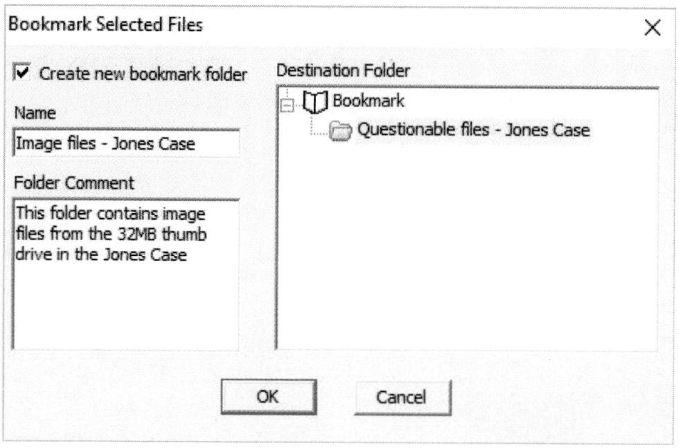

Bookmark Selected Files   ×

☑ Create new bookmark folder   Destination Folder

Name   ⊟ 📖 Bookmark

Image files - Jones Case   📁 Questionable files - Jones Case

Folder Comment

This folder contains image
files from the 32MB thumb
drive in the Jones Case

OK   Cancel

Source: EnCase

Figure 3-15   Bookmark folders allow an investigator to organize bookmarks.

Adding Bookmarks

An investigator can add a bookmark by right-clicking on any file and selecting **Bookmark Files.**

Bookmarking a Selected Area

An investigator can bookmark a selected area by highlighting the text area and selecting **Bookmark Data,** as shown in Figure 3-16.

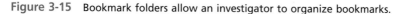

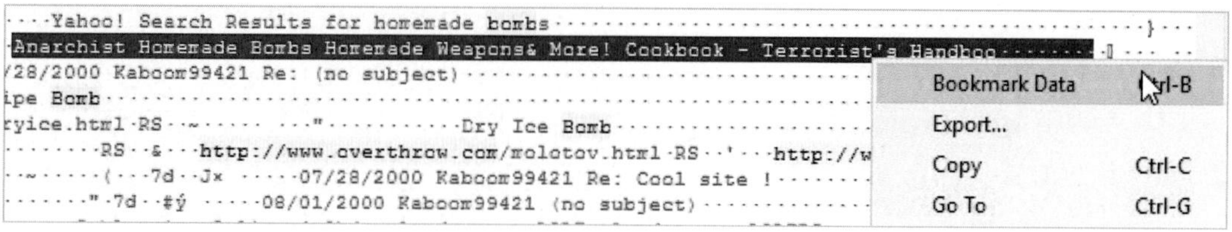

····Yahoo! Search Results for homemade bombs·····························}···
Anarchist Homemade Bombs Homemade Weapons& More! Cookbook - Terrorist's Handboo·······]····
/28/2000 Kaboom99421 Re: (no subject)···································
ipe Bomb··   Bookmark Data   Ctrl-B
ryice.html·RS··~·····"···········Dry Ice Bomb····················
·······RS··&···http://www.overthrow.com/molotov.html·RS··'··http://w   Export...
·~·······(···7d··Jx····07/28/2000 Kaboom99421 Re: Cool site !·······   Copy   Ctrl-C
······"·7d··£ý·····08/01/2000 Kaboom99421 (no subject)··········   Go To   Ctrl-G

Source: EnCase

Figure 3-16   An investigator can bookmark an area of text.

Recovering Deleted Files/Folders in a FAT Partition

An investigator can recover deleted files and folders by right-clicking a FAT drive and selecting **Recover Folders,** as shown in Figures 3-17 and 3-18.

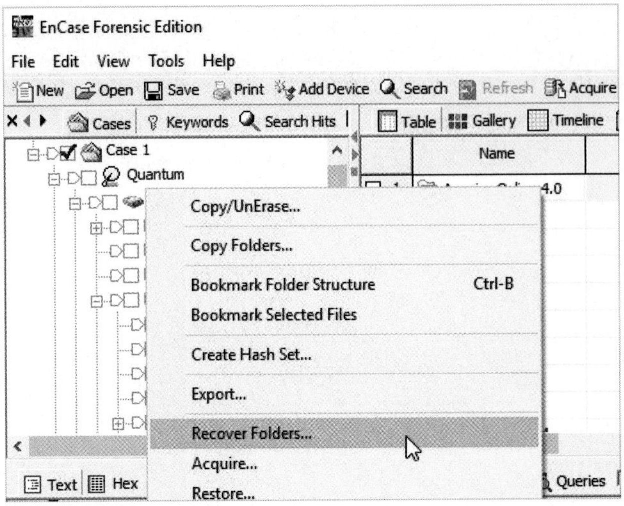

Source: EnCase

Figure 3-17 EnCase allows an investigator to recover deleted files and folders.

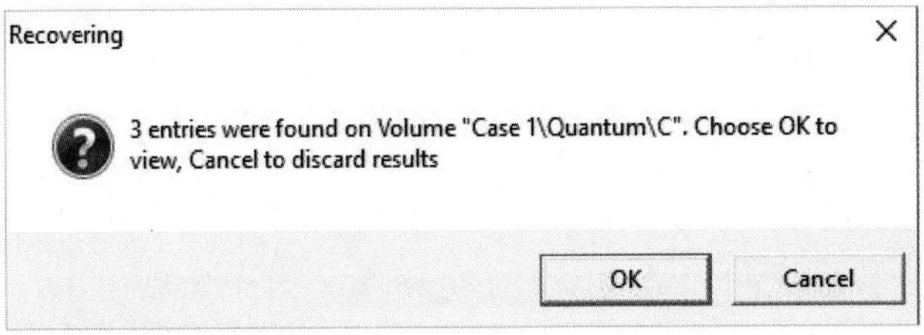

Source: EnCase

Figure 3-18 An investigator can view the file and folder recovery results or discard them.

Viewing Recovered Files

An investigator can select the **Recovered Folder** to view the deleted files and folders that have been recovered, as shown in Figure 3-19.

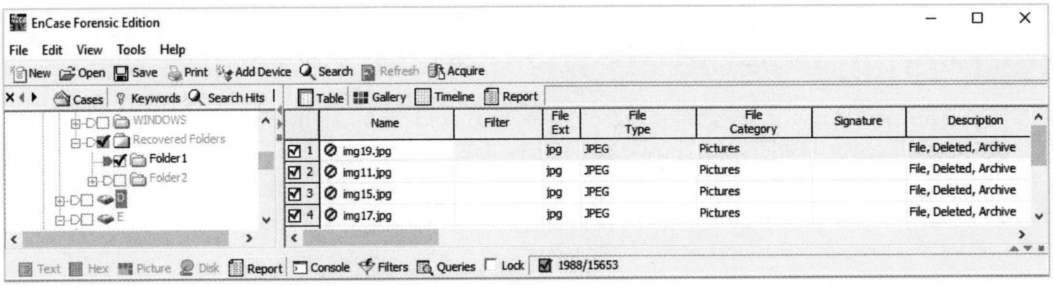

Source: EnCase

Figure 3-19 The **Recovered Folder** shows the files and folders that EnCase has recovered.

Recovering Files/Folders in an NTFS Partition

EnCase searches unallocated clusters in the master file table (MFT) to recover files and folders. It uses a similar recovery method with an NTFS partition as it does with an FAT partition.

EnCase automatically rebuilds the structure of the formatted NTFS. It automatically searches the drive and finds artifacts from the previous partition. The partition information, directory structure, and folder structure are then automatically rebuilt. This capability is of critical importance in cases where a machine has been repurposed to another employee in the organization. If an individual who is the subject of an investigation used a repurposed machine, an investigator would need to recover the files from the previous NTFS volume.

The folder recovery process can be slow and may take 60 minutes (1 hour) for 100-GB hard drives.

The following are the steps to recover folders on an NTFS partition:

1. Right-click on the volume and select **Recover Folders**.
2. Choose **OK** to begin the search for NTFS folders.

Master Boot Record (MBR)

The master boot record (MBR) resides at the first sector (sector 0). The sector offset (SO) 446 contains the partition table.

The MBR allows four entries:

- Each entry is 16 bytes long.
- Partition entries range from LE 64 to 55 AA.

The following are the steps for checking MBR entries:

1. Select sectors SO 446 to LE 64 (Figure 3-20).
2. Right-click and select **Bookmark**.
3. Select **Windows** and then **Partition Entry**.
4. Enter a name for the bookmark.

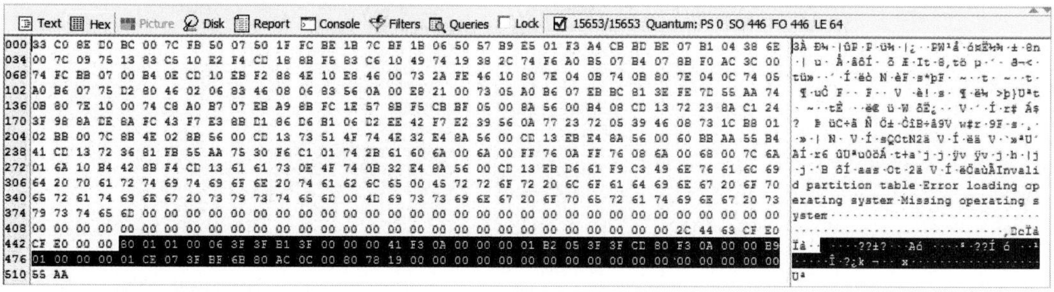

Figure 3-20 An investigator can bookmark the MBR.

NTFS Starting Point

Track 0 is normally considered the first 63 sectors of a disk and is reserved for the MBR. The MBR holds the partition table and the default Microsoft bootstrap code.

NTFS partitioning rules start the first primary partition in the 64th sector, as shown in Figure 3-21.

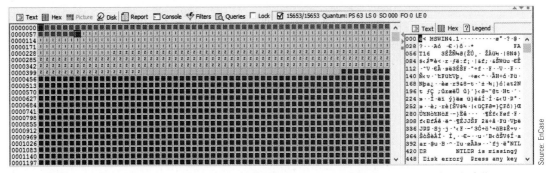

Figure 3-21 The first primary partition on an NTFS disk starts in the 64th sector, immediately following the MBR.

Viewing Disk Geometry

An investigator can view disk geometry by highlighting the case and clicking **Report** on the top menu, as shown in Figure 3-22.

Name:	Quantum
Description:	Physical Disk, 2503872 Sectors, 1.2GB
Logical Size:	0
Physical Size:	512
Starting Extent:	0S0
Physical Location:	0
Evidence File:	Quantum
Full Path:	Case 1\Quantum

Device

Evidence Number:	2000-18-2
File Path:	E:\Encase Evidence E01 Files\Quantum1.E01
Examiner Name:	Sheldon
Actual Date:	08/13/00 08:53:29AM
Target Date:	08/13/00 08:53:29AM
Total Size:	1,281,982,464 bytes (1.2GB)
Total Sectors:	2,503,872
CHS:	2484:16:63
File Integrity:	Completely Verified, 0 Errors
Acquisition Hash:	7F2232072D72F2ED8167581063573326
Verify Hash:	7F2232072D72F2ED8167581063573326
Notes:	Copyright 2000 Guidance Software, Inc.

Partitions

Code	Type	Start Sector	Total Sectors	Size
06	BIGDOS	0	717,696	350.4MB
07	NTFS	830,592	1,669,248	815.1MB
06	BIGDOS	717,696	112,896	55.1MB

Source: EnCase

Figure 3-22 The **Report** tab shows the disk geometry of all devices in a case.

Recovering Deleted Partitions

There are two ways to check for deleted partitions:

1. Search for the following in the unused disk area:
   a. MSWIN4.1 (FAT partition)
   b. NTFS (NTFS partition)
2. Look manually on the disk at the end of the first volume.

An investigator can recover the partition by right-clicking the area to recover and selecting **Add Partition,** as shown in Figure 3-23. An investigator can delete a partition by right-clicking and selecting **Remove user defined partitions.**

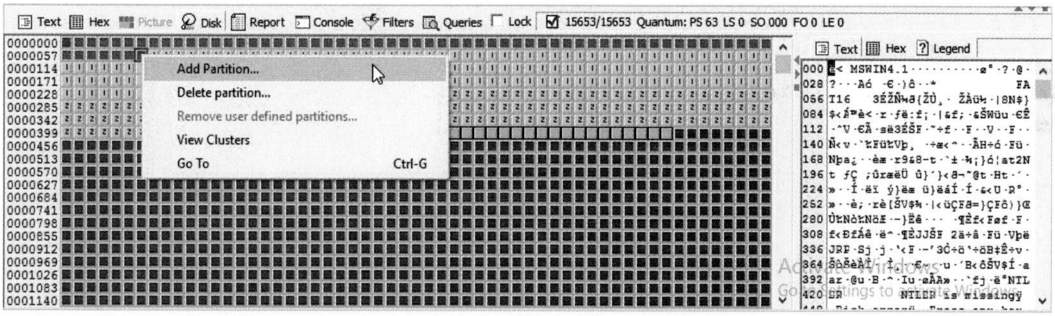

Source: EnCase

Figure 3-23 An investigator can recover deleted FAT and NTFS partitions.

Hash Values

Figure 3-24 shows a list of hash values for the files in a case.

	Name	Hash Value
818	bombs.htm	1b37a418f6b27ce1a4ccd47b598f47b4
819	ACOOK.TXT	8f1d9f592b6d256612da22ea0347b75d
820	fire19-96.jpg	1fd76010b76073cde3461e1309a15b1e
821	22bomb.txt	ea10405f71d68151aaa54a80238f6961
822	Re Interesting Phe...	7028e8a664a585caebf598aac2f83690
823	anarchy.htm	3da0c5b6362f9f307a0354a0c0248757
824	anarcook.txt	76d50c978feb3494b84c2b4b97dfebfd

Source: EnCase

Figure 3-24 EnCase hashes files to help in verifying file integrity.

Creating Hash Sets

An investigator can create a hash set by performing the following steps:

1. Select the files to be included in the hash set.

2. Right-click and choose **Create Hash Set** (Figure 3-25).

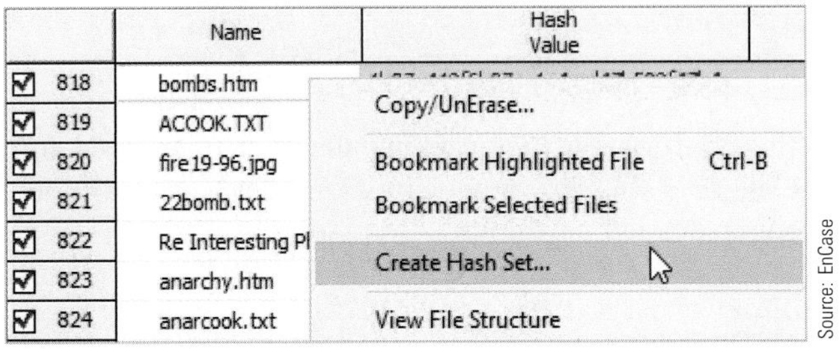

		Name	Hash Value
☑	818	bombs.htm	
☑	819	ACOOK.TXT	Copy/UnErase...
☑	820	fire 19-96.jpg	Bookmark Highlighted File Ctrl-B
☑	821	22bomb.txt	Bookmark Selected Files
☑	822	Re Interesting Pl	
☑	823	anarchy.htm	Create Hash Set...
☑	824	anarcook.txt	View File Structure

Source: EnCase

Figure 3-25   Hash sets allow an investigator to organize hash values.

MD5 Hash

The MD5 hash is a 128-bit (16-byte) value that uniquely describes the contents of a file. It is a one-way hash function that converts a message into a fixed string of digits called message digests.

The purpose of the value within EnCase is to verify that the evidence file EnCase created is the same in byte structure as the original media. EnCase also uses MD5 hashing to create hash sets that are then added to the hash library. Hash sets are collections of hash files.

EnCase can create a hash value (digital fingerprint) for any file in the case.

The chance of two files having the same hash value is 2^{-128}. The likelihood of duplication in MD5 is 340,282,366,920,938,463,463,374,607,431,768,211,456 to 1.

Creating Hashes

An investigator can click **Search** and select **Compute Hash Value** to create a hash for every allocated file. Figure 3-26 shows computed hash values for a set of files in the right column.

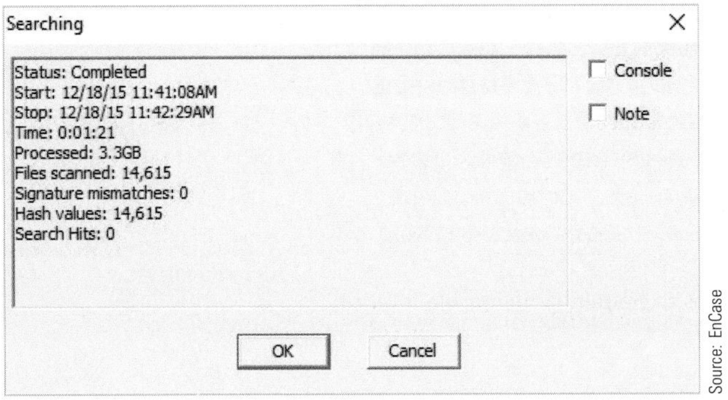

```
Searching                                                    ✕

Status: Completed                              ☐ Console
Start: 12/18/15 11:41:08AM
Stop: 12/18/15 11:42:29AM                      ☐ Note
Time: 0:01:21
Processed: 3.3GB
Files scanned: 14,615
Signature mismatches: 0
Hash values: 14,615
Search Hits: 0




            [ OK ]        [ Cancel ]
```

Source: EnCase

Figure 3-26   An investigator can easily create hash values for every file in a case.

Viewers

EnCase allows an investigator to use external viewers to view files. EnCase will copy a file to a temporary folder before launching the viewer to display the file. EnCase can use the following types of viewers:

- *External viewer*: EnCase can be enhanced quickly to use external file viewers, easing the analysis of foreign file types, and allowing for the use of native applications from the source machine.

- *Registry viewer*: The integrated registry viewer organizes the registry data file into folders, giving examiners an expedient and efficient way to view the Windows registry and determine values.

- *EnCase viewer*: The fully integrated picture viewer automatically locates and displays many known graphical image types, including Microsoft thumbs.db files.

- *Timeline*: This integrated viewer allows an examiner to see all relevant time attributes of all the files in the case (or selected group of files) in a powerful graphical environment.

An investigator can see the viewers by clicking **Viewers** in the **View** menu. The investigator can create a new viewer just by entering the application path.

Signature Analysis

The ISO (International Organization for Standardization) and ITU (International Telecommunication Union) work to standardize types of electronic data. When a file type becomes standardized, a signature or header is stored along with the data. Applications use the header to correctly parse the data. An investigator can view the file signature to identify the file type, even if its extension has been changed.

To perform signature analysis, an investigator can select **View** and then **File Signatures**.

Viewing the Results

Figure 3-27 shows the results of signature analysis.

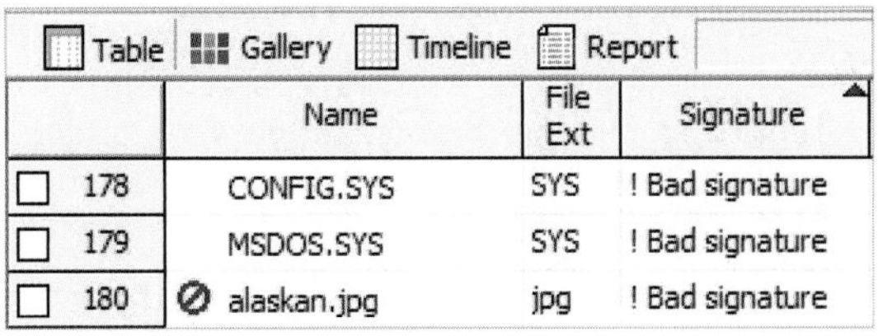

		Name	File Ext	Signature
☐	178	CONFIG.SYS	SYS	! Bad signature
☐	179	MSDOS.SYS	SYS	! Bad signature
☐	180	⊘ alaskan.jpg	jpg	! Bad signature

Figure 3-27   EnCase displays the results of signature analysis once it has completed the task.

Copying Files and Folders

An investigator can select a group of files and folders to copy, as shown in Figure 3-28. The investigator can unerase the file if EnCase indicates that it has been deleted.

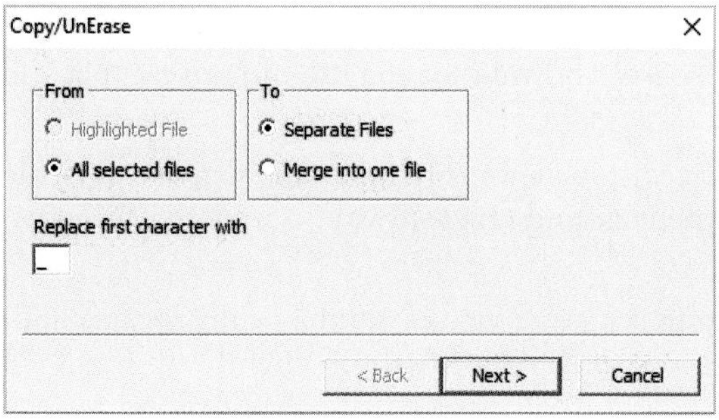

Figure 3-28   An investigator can copy and unerase files and folders.

E-Mail Recovery

The default path for Outlook Express 5/6 in Windows XP is \Documents and Settings\<username>\Local Settings\Application Data\Identities\<userid>\Microsoft\Outlook Express.

The following are the Outlook mailbox file names:

- Inbox.mbx
- Outbox.mbx
- Sent Items.mbx
- Deleted Items.mbx
- Drafts.mbx

An investigator can view these files in EnCase.

Reporting

The final stage of forensic analysis is reporting. A report must be easy to understand and cover in-depth information about the evidence. To create a report, an investigator can click **Report** in the **Bookmarks** menu. Figure 3-29 shows a final report.

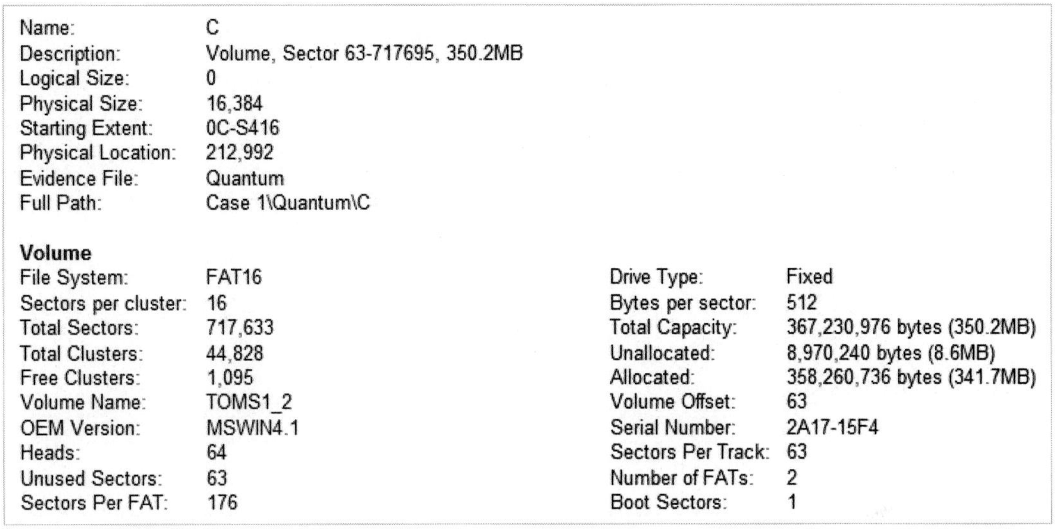

```
Name:                 C
Description:          Volume, Sector 63-717695, 350.2MB
Logical Size:         0
Physical Size:        16,384
Starting Extent:      0C-S416
Physical Location:    212,992
Evidence File:        Quantum
Full Path:            Case 1\Quantum\C
```

Volume

File System:	FAT16	Drive Type:	Fixed
Sectors per cluster:	16	Bytes per sector:	512
Total Sectors:	717,633	Total Capacity:	367,230,976 bytes (350.2MB)
Total Clusters:	44,828	Unallocated:	8,970,240 bytes (8.6MB)
Free Clusters:	1,095	Allocated:	358,260,736 bytes (341.7MB)
Volume Name:	TOMS1_2	Volume Offset:	63
OEM Version:	MSWIN4.1	Serial Number:	2A17-15F4
Heads:	64	Sectors Per Track:	63
Unused Sectors:	63	Number of FATs:	2
Sectors Per FAT:	176	Boot Sectors:	1

Source: EnCase

Figure 3-29   The final report shows the analysis results for a case.

EnCase Boot Disks

An investigator can create a boot disk directly in EnCase. The investigator can use this boot disk to boot up in MS-DOS mode. By using this disk, he or she can create bitstream images. Figure 3-30 shows EnCase creating a boot disk.

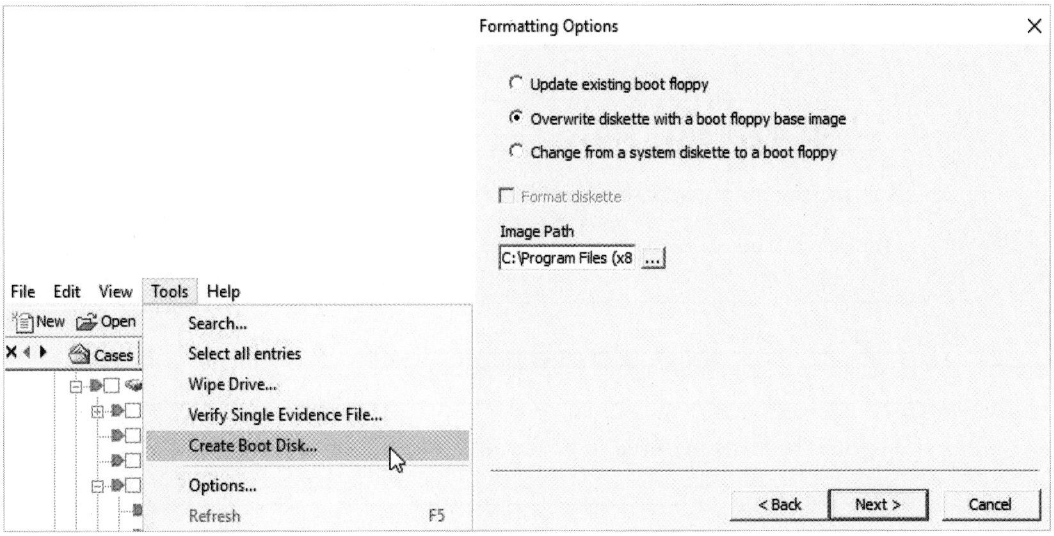

Figure 3-30   An investigator can use an EnCase boot disk to create a bitstream image of a device.

Chapter Summary

- The evidence file is the core component in EnCase.
- Each evidence file is an exact sector-by-sector copy of a floppy or hard disk.
- EnCase calculates an MD5 hash when it acquires a physical drive or logical drive.
- EnCase provides powerful searching capabilities.
- EnCase allows an investigator to bookmark files, folders, or sections of a file for easy reference.
- EnCase searches unallocated clusters in the master file table (MFT) to recover files and folders.
- EnCase can create a hash value (digital fingerprint) for any file in a case.

Key Terms

cyclic redundancy check (CRC)   checksum   hashing

Review Questions

1. What is an EnCase evidence file, and what is it used for?

   _____

   _____

   _____

   _____

2. Describe the main parts of an evidence file.

   _____

   _____

   _____

   _____

3. Describe the steps involved in acquiring an image of a storage device.

   _____

   _____

   _____

   _____

4. What does the **Device** tab show?

    _____

    _____

    _____

    _____

3

5. What is the purpose of an EnCase boot disk?

    _____

    _____

    _____

    _____

6. What is the purpose of file-signature analysis?

    _____

    _____

    _____

    _____

7. How does EnCase use MD5 hashing?

    _____

    _____

    _____

    _____

8. Describe the kinds of searches an investigator can perform using EnCase.

    _____

    _____

    _____

    _____

Hands-On Projects

1. Install Encase and create a case file structure:
   - Navigate to Chapter 3 in MindTap or on the Student Resource Center.
   - Download the "Installer for Encase".
   - Unzip and double-click the "**setup**" file to install the Encase program.
   - Click "**Install Encase**" (Figure 3-31).

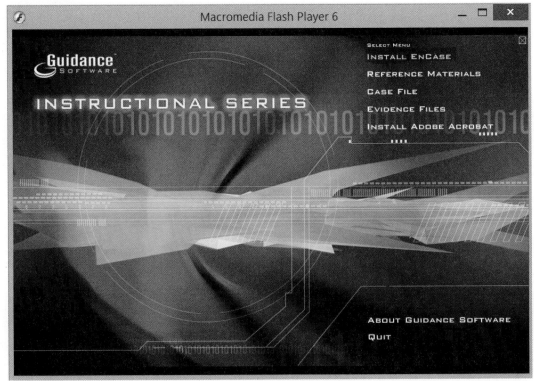

Figure 3-31 EnCase "Install" window.

- Follow the on-screen instructions to complete the installation.
- Create a subfolder on your desktop called "MyCases".
- Create a subfolder in MyCases called "Case1".
- Create three subfolders in Case1 called "evidence", "temp", and "export".
- Start EnCase and select "**File**", "**New**".
- Enter your name in the "Examiner Name" field.
- Click the browse button to change the Export folder to "MyCases\Case1\export".

- Click the browse button to change the Temporary folder to "MyCases\Case1\temp".
- Click "**Finish**" (Figure 3-32).

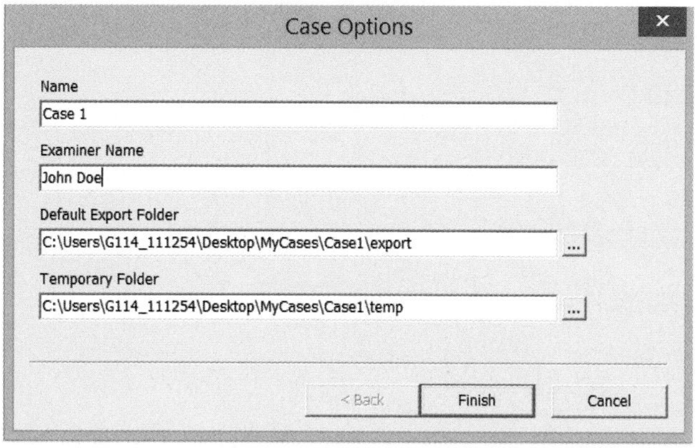

Figure 3-32 EnCase "Case Options" field information for Case 1.

- Select "**File**", "**Save**", browse to "MyCases\Case1" and save as "Case 1".
- You now have the file structure necessary to support an entire forensic investigation.
- Prepare a one-paragraph summary detailing your efforts, include screenshots where appropriate.

2. Examine a case file in EnCase for specific keywords:
   - Create a case file structure for the StudentDemo case:
     ◦ Create a subfolder in MyCases called "StudentDemo".
     ◦ Create three subfolders in StudentDemo called "evidence", "temp", and "export".
   - Download and open a case in EnCase and set the options.
     ◦ Navigate to Chapter 3 in MindTap or on the Student Resource Center.
     ◦ Download the "Encase Evidence Files".
     ◦ Unzip and copy all five files into the "MyCases\StudentDemo\evidence" folder.
     ◦ Locate "MyCases\StudentDemo\evidence\Quantum1", right-click and select "**Open**" to open the file in Encase.

- ◦ Enter "StudentDemo" as the Name, fill in the remaining information in each field and click "**Finish**" (Figure 3-33).

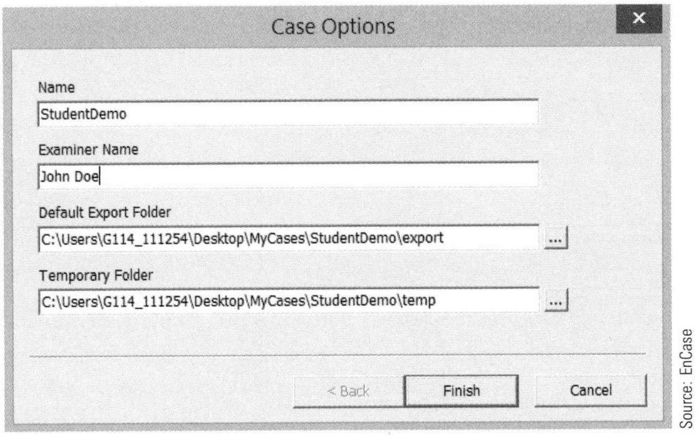

Figure 3-33   EnCase "Case Options" field information for StudentDemo.

- ◦ Select "**File**", "**Save**", browse to "MyCases\StudentDemo" and save as "StudentDemo".
- Search for specific keywords in the StudentDemo case in EnCase:
  - ◦ Note the three panes:
    - ▪ Left – contains evidence file listings.
    - ▪ Right – contains folders and subfolders within the selected evidence file.
    - ▪ Bottom – contains the contents of the selected file structure (Figure 3-34).

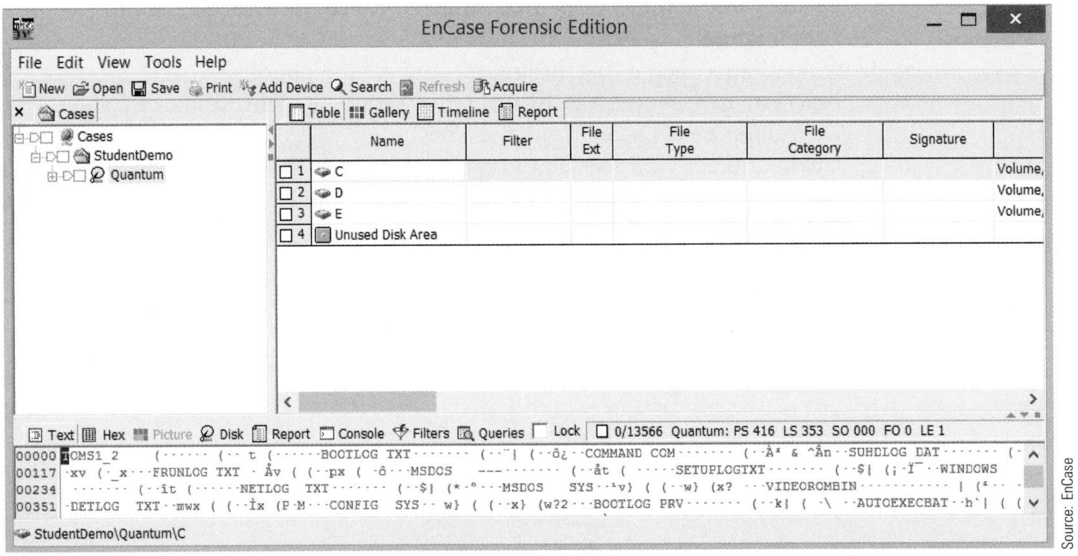

Figure 3-34   EnCase "left", "right", and "bottom" panes.

- In the left pane, expand "**Quantum**", then expand "**C:**", and then select "**My Documents.**" Notice that 22 files are in the right pane when My Documents is selected.
- In the left pane, click the pentagon symbol in front of "My Documents". This is the "All Files" button to display all the files within all of the folders in the selected folder. Notice that 1,437 files are now displayed in the right pane.
- Click the checkbox to select the "My Documents" folder.
- Select "**View**", "**Keywords**".
- In the left pane, right-click the "**Keywords**" folder, and select "**Add Keyword List**".
- Add the following keywords on individual lines: "investigator", "search warrant", "reports", "victim", "bomb", "explosion", "fire", "gun", and "pain".
- Check "Active Code-Page" and click "**OK**". Active Code-Page assists in identifying the language.
- Click the "**Search**" button (Figure 3-35).

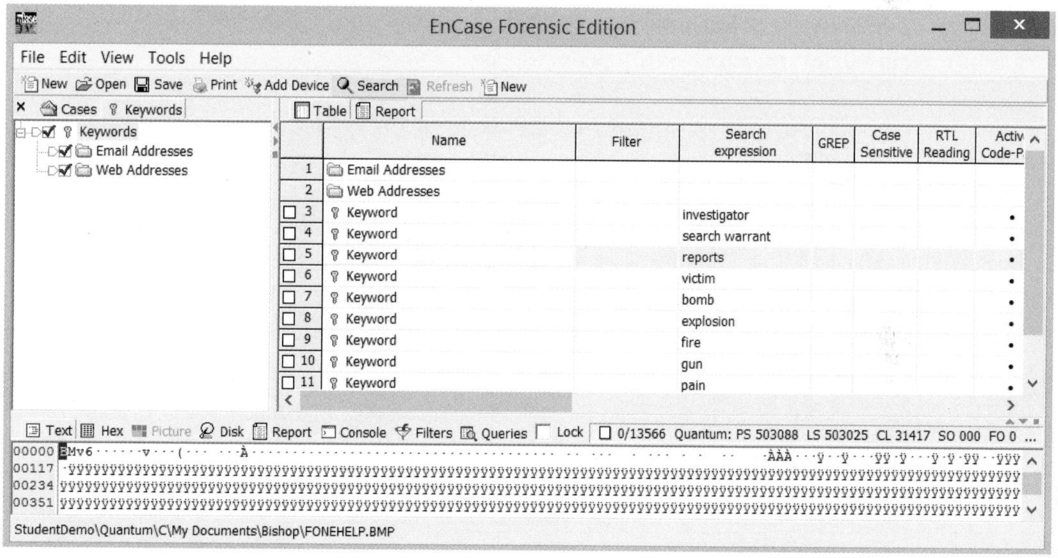

Figure 3-35   EnCase "Search" button.

○ Check "**Selected Files Only**" and click "**Start**" (Figure 3-36).

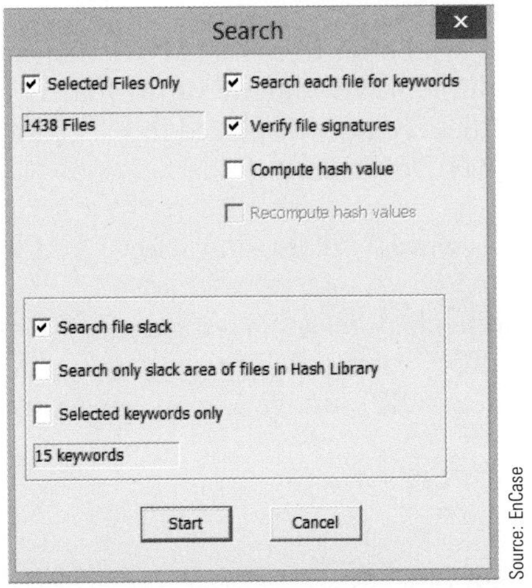

Figure 3-36 EnCase "Search" options window.

○ Note the progress bar at the bottom of the screen showing the estimated time to completion.
○ The search cannot be interrupted once started.
○ Upon completion, the summary screen will display, click "**OK**" (Figure 3-37).

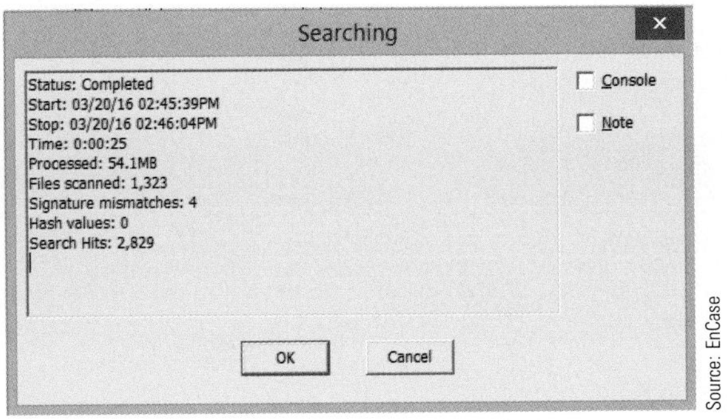

Figure 3-37 EnCase "Searching" summary results window.

- Click "**View**", "**Search Hits**" to review the search results.
- In the left pane, select the word "**bomb**" to view the contextual hits in the right pane (Figure 3-38).

Source: EnCase

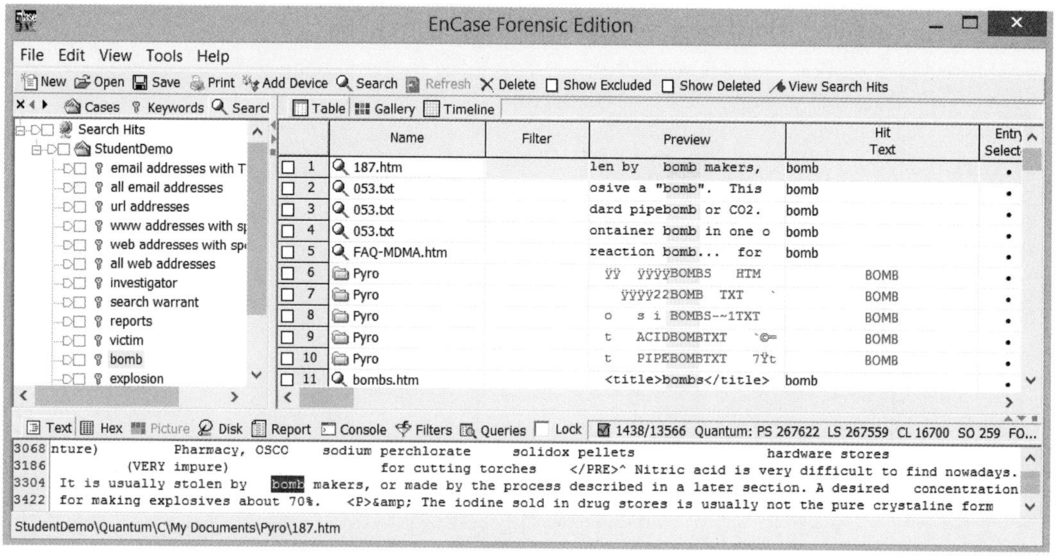

Figure 3-38 EnCase contextual hits on keyword "bomb".

- In the right pane, locate search result #387, with the filename "tth2.txt". Select this result and review the contents in the bottom pane.
- Prepare a one-paragraph summary detailing your efforts and the benefits of the EnCase Keyword Search feature in a forensic investigation.

3. Explore the EnCase "QuickStart Manual" and identify and test additional functionality:
   - When you downloaded the "Installer for EnCase" in Hands-on Project 1 of this chapter, the zip file also contained a pdf titled "QuickStart Manual" (Figure 3-39). Locate and open this pdf.

Source: EnCase

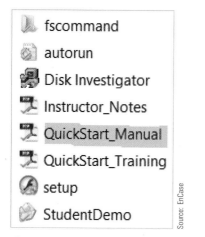

Figure 3-39 EnCase "QuickStart_Manual" in Windows Explorer.

- Review the documentation in the "QuickStart Manual" and identify a feature, in addition to the Keyword Search, that would be useful in a forensic investigation.
- Test out the feature, using EnCase, on the StudentDemo case.
- Prepare a one-paragraph summary identifying the EnCase feature you tested and the results yielded from your efforts.

chapter 4

Recovering Deleted Files and Deleted Partitions

After completing this chapter, you should be able to:

- Delete files
- Understand what happens when a file is deleted
- Understand the Recycle Bin
- Perform data recovery in Linux
- Know and understand data recovery tools
- Delete partitions
- Recover deleted partitions
- Know and understand partition recovery tools

What If?

William Hickey, a 44-year-old Mingus Union High School teacher, was suspected of downloading child pornography onto the school's computer, but no charges were filed against him.

Though Hickey had tendered his resignation, he was allowed to work from home until his resignation went into effect on December 22, 2006. Police seized the computer and sent it to the Department of Public Safety. There, police investigated whether it contained images of child pornography. They did locate some pornographic images but have not identified any potential victims. It was reported, however, that the forensic investigation could take weeks, or even months, to conduct tests.

- What program could the investigator use to look for deleted files and images?
- How would the investigators prove the existence of any deleted images for the case?

Introduction to Recovering Deleted Files and Deleted Partitions

This chapter focuses on recovering deleted files and deleted partitions. It begins by covering deleting files and the Recycle Bin. It then moves on to the subject of file recovery, including file recovery in Linux and the file recovery tools that forensic investigators use. The chapter then discusses deleting and recovering partitions. It finishes with an overview of partition recovery tools.

Deleting Files

There are different ways to delete files, depending on the file system and operating system a computer is using. On a Windows system, most deleted files are sent to the Recycle Bin. The **Recycle Bin** is a space on a disk for files and folders that are marked for deletion. The following steps show one way to delete files by moving them to the Recycle Bin:

- Right-click on the file or folder you want to remove, and choose the **Delete** option in the context menu.
- Windows will confirm that you wish to send the file to the Recycle Bin.

There are other options for deleting files on a Windows computer:

- Select the file or folder you want to delete, and press the Delete key on the keyboard.
- Select the file or folder you want to delete. Go to the taskbar option **File** and click **Delete**.
- Drag and drop files into the Recycle Bin.

What Happens When a File Is Deleted in Windows?

When a user deletes a file, the operating system does not actually erase the file. It marks the file name in the master file table (MFT) with a special character that tells the processor that the file has been deleted.

The operating system replaces the first letter of a deleted file name with a hex byte code: E5h. E5h is a special tag that indicates that the file has been deleted. The corresponding cluster of that file in FAT is marked as unused, though it will continue to contain the information until it is overwritten.

The Recycle Bin in Windows

The Recycle Bin is located on the Windows desktop. When a user deletes an item from the hard disk, the Recycle Bin icon changes from empty to full. However, this item has not actually been erased. It is tagged as information to be deleted. When the user empties the Recycle Bin, he or she is telling the computer that the space those files used is now free to store new information.

Items deleted from removable media, such as a flash memory card or network drive, are not actually stored in the Recycle Bin. When a user ejects the removable media, he or she will no longer be able to access the files he or she deleted or moved to the Recycle Bin. The items present in the Recycle Bin still take up dedicated, adjustable space on the hard disk. These items can be restored to their original positions with the help of the **Restore all items** option of the Recycle Bin. After being deleted from the Recycle Bin, these items still take up space in the hard disk until the operating system overwrites the location where the information is stored.

When the Recycle Bin becomes full, Windows automatically deletes the older items. Because the Recycle Bin takes up a specific space on each partition of the hard disk, very large items are not stored in the Recycle Bin. They are deleted permanently.

A user can manipulate the Recycle Bin in a number of ways. The following steps show how to change the storage capacity of the Recycle Bin:

- Right-click on **Recycle Bin** and choose **Properties**.
- Increase or decrease the storage capacity by moving the bar.

The following steps show how to restore files in the Recycle Bin:

- Open Recycle Bin.
- Right-click the item to restore. Then choose **Restore**.

It is possible to select more than one item to restore. Select the items to restore, and choose **Restore All**.

The following steps show how to delete files in the Recycle Bin:

- Open Recycle Bin.
- Right-click the file to delete, and choose **Delete**.

Storage Location of Recycle Bin in FAT and NTFS
On an FAT drive, deleted files are stored in the location C:\RECYCLED; on an NTFS drive, files are stored in the C:\RECYCLER folder.

The Recycle Bin folders in FAT and NTFS have two different names to avoid confusion, in case a computer system has both file systems, or a file system is converted to another file system, as when FAT is converted to NTFS.

FAT and NTFS Recycle Bins have different internal structures. All recycled files in the FAT system are dumped into a single C:\RECYCLED directory, while recycled files on the NTFS system are categorized into directories named as C:\RECYCLER\S- . . . ., based on the user's Windows **security identifier (SID)**.

By default, the Recycle Bin was 10 percent of the user's quota on the volume in Windows XP. In later versions of Windows, the default size is 10 percent of the first 40 GB of quota, and 5 percent of any quota above 40 GB. Items that exceed the capacity of the Recycle Bin are deleted immediately.

How the Recycle Bin Works   Each hard disk has a hidden folder named Recycled. This folder contains the files deleted from Windows Explorer or My Computer.

Deleted files are stored in the **Recycled folder**. Each deleted file in the folder is renamed. A hidden file called INFO2 holds the original names and paths. This information is used to restore the deleted files to their original locations.

The syntax for renaming is the following: Dxy.ext.

- All recycled files begin with the letter D; D denotes that a file has been deleted.
- The second letter (x) is the letter of the drive where the file is located. If the file resides on the main hard drive, it will be the letter C. If it is on the floppy drive, it will be the letter A.
- The final piece (y) denotes a sequential number starting from 0.
- The file will keep the same extension as the original file, such as .doc or .pdf.

Consider the following example:

- *New file name*: Dc1.txt = (C drive, second file deleted, a .txt file)
- *INFO2 file path*: C:\Windows\Desktop\Forensics.txt
- *New file name*: De7.doc = (E drive, eighth file deleted, a .doc file)
- *INFO2 file path*: E:\Homework\James Joyce Essay.doc

Damaged or Deleted INFO2 File   Once the INFO2 file is damaged or deleted, it will not appear in the Recycle Bin, but the deleted renamed files will still be present in the Recycled folder. Because the files were renamed in the Recycled folder, but not changed, they can be searched and restored by locating the file based on the new naming convention and renaming the file.

When the INFO2 file is deleted, it will be re-created when a user restarts Windows. If the Recycle Bin is damaged and not working, the user must delete the hidden INFO2 file from the Recycled folder and restart Windows to re-create the INFO2 file; this will enable the user to access the deleted files in the Recycle Bin. A user can also delete the INFO2 file from a command prompt window:

- cd recycled
- attrib -h inf*
- del info

Damaged Files in the Recycled Folder

Damaged or deleted files will not appear in the Recycle Bin. In such cases, follow the steps below to recover the deleted files:

- Make a copy of the **Recycled\Desktop.ini** file in a separate folder, and delete all the contents from the Recycled folder.
- Delete all files in the Recycle Bin.

- Restore the Desktop.ini file to the Recycled folder.
- If there is no Desktop.ini file or if it is damaged, re-create it by adding the following information to a new Desktop.ini file:

```
[.ShellClassInfo]
  CLSID={645FF040-5081-101B-9F08-00AA002F954E}
```

Damaged Recycled Folder

At times, the Recycled folder itself can be damaged. In this case, a user will still be able to send files to the Recycled folder, even though the Recycle Bin on the desktop appears full. The user will not be able to view the contents of the Recycle Bin, and the **Empty Recycle Bin** command will also be unavailable.

To fix this, a user needs to delete the Recycled folder and restart Windows; Windows will regenerate the folder and restore its functionality.

The Recycled folder can also be generated from the command prompt:

- attrib -s -h recycled
- del recycled

Close the command window and restart the computer.

How to Undelete a File

If a file has been deleted from the Recycle Bin, in order to fully or partially restore it, a user will have to **undelete** the file. The process of file undeletion involves locating the data on the disk partitions and allowing the operating system to access the file. There are two main ways of carrying this out:

- Modify the existing file system to remove the "deleted" flag from the file to restore it.
- Locate the data in the partition, and copy it to a new file.

Data Recovery in Linux

The main advantage that Linux has over Windows is its ability to access and recover data from otherwise problematic machines. All file systems are supported in a standard stock kernel, which should have the ability to support older file systems. Therefore, the Linux kernel supports a large number of file systems, including VxFS, UFS, HFS, and the aforementioned NTFS and FAT systems. Note that Mac OS X is based on OpenBSD and thus uses the same UNIX/Linux kernel.

Individuals can, in some cases, dual-boot Linux and Windows; this can be done by using FAT and NTFS. Data of machines that fail to boot in a Windows environment can easily be recovered using bootable Linux, such as Knoppix.

In Linux, files that are deleted using the command /bin/rm remain on the disk. If a running process keeps a file open and then removes the file, the file contents are still on the disk, and other programs will not reclaim the space. The second extended file system (ext2) is commonly used in most Linux systems. The design of ext2 is such that it shows several places where data can be hidden.

It is worthwhile to note that if an executable erases itself, its contents can be retrieved from a /proc memory image. The command cp /proc/$PID/exe/tmp/file creates a copy of a file in /tmp.

Tools to Recover Deleted Files
File Recovery Tools for Windows

Tool: Active@ UNDELETE 10

Operating Systems: Supports Windows 8, 7, Vista, XP and Windows
Servers 2003, 2008
File Types: All
Media: Hard drives, including RAID arrays, and removable media
Web Site: *http://www.active-undelete.com/*
Cost: $19.99

Active@ UNDELETE is a powerful data recovery software that helps a user recover lost, deleted, and formatted data from hard drives, floppy disks, basic and dynamic volumes, hardware or software RAID (RAID0 and RAID5). It supports compressed, encrypted, and fragmented files. Besides hard disk drives and floppies, the program supports recovery from removable devices such as Secure Digital, CompactFlash, SmartMedia, Sony Memory Stick, Zip drives, and USB hard drives.

Active@ UNDELETE recovers lost files formatted in NTFS, FAT, FAT32, exFAT, HFS+, ext2/ext3/ext4, and UFS file systems, and it works under all Windows family operating systems: Windows 8/Windows 7/Vista/Windows XP, Windows 2003/2008 Servers. Active@ UNDELETE incorporates many wizards that provide expert users full control over the process of data restoration.

The following are some of the features of Active@ UNDELETE:

- Recovers files on IDE/ATA/SATA/SCSI hard disk drives
- Recovers files on removable devices (SmartMedia, Secure Digital, Memory Stick, and so on.)
- Supports external Zip drives and USB hard drives
- Recovers files from deleted, damaged, formatted, or reformatted partitions
- Supports NTFS, FAT, FAT32, exFAT, HFS+, ext2/ext3/ext4, UFS file systems
- Supports recovery of compressed, fragmented, and encrypted files on NTFS
- Advanced search by file name, file date, mask, size range, and attributes
- Two types of drive and device scan: Basic (fast) and Thorough (slow)
- Ability to create and work with raw and compressed disk images representing the whole drive in one file
- Ability to connect to remote machines and scan, create disk images, and recover data remotely
- Supports hardware and software RAID

Tool: Active@ UNERASER

Operating Systems: DOS and Windows
File Types: All
Media: Hard drives and floppy disks
Web Site: *http://www.uneraser.com/*
Cost: Freeware Version: Free
Professional Version: $39.99

4

Active@ UNERASER is powerful hard drive recovery software for DOS and Windows (Console) that can recover deleted files and folders and volumes on NTFS, FAT, exFAT, Linux ext2/ext3/ext4/BtrFS, Apple HFS+ and Unix UFS/ZFS. It can even restore files from deleted and reformatted partitions.

With this data recovery software, NTFS drives can be recognized and deleted items can be recovered while working from the DOS and Windows (Console) environment. It is not necessary to install the utility on a hard drive, as it fits on a bootable floppy disk, removing the possibility of overwriting the data a user wants to recover.

Freeware version allows using most products' capabilities and performing basic recovery tasks. Most disk problems can be easily solved with it, like an unerase of accidentally deleted files or recovering files on a volume being damaged by a virus or power surge.

Professional versions of Active@ UNERASER:

- Do not contain limitations on the number of files being recovered per one recovery session
- Option to recover partition/volume "in-place" or to copy all volume data to a new disk
- Boot Disk Creator prepares USB/CD/DVD bootable media to recover unbootable systems
- Included—Active@ Boot Disk and Active@ LiveCD—recovery environments to boot into
- Boot Disk contains these tools: File and Partition Managers, Disk Monitor, Networking
- Boot Disk boots up the latest UEFI x86 (32-bit) and x64 (64-bit) secure boot systems
- Able to repair infected systems: antivirus scanner can download the latest virus database

The following are some of the features of Active@ UNERASER:

- Recovers lost data on all DOS/Windows systems, whether FAT or NTFS partitions
- Undeletes compressed, fragmented, sparse, and encrypted files on NTFS
- Recovers deleted files with long or non-English file names
- Unformats (i.e., recovers) files from formatted hard drives
- Creates and works with raw and compressed drive images for backup purposes
- Unerases files from deleted and damaged partitions and logical drives
- Scans hard drives and displays deleted FAT and NTFS partitions and/or logical drives
- Views files and any sector contents in hex/text viewer
- Supports LBA mode for access to large hard drives

- Two types of drive and device scan: Basic (fast) and Thorough (slow)
- Full support for long and localized file names for display and recovery
- Extended file and drive attributes support for information display
- Encrypting File System (EFS) support in Windows (Console) application
- Advanced searching: by mask, size, attribute, deleted/existing only
- Advanced disk imaging: raw and compressed disk images, composing disk images from raw chunks (created by other tools), and checking disk image consistency
- Read and copy existing files from NTFS to FAT partition

Tool: Recover My Files

Operating Systems: Windows
File Types: All
Media: Hard drives
Web Site: *http://www.recovermyfiles.com/*
Cost: $69.95

Recover My Files data recovery software will recover deleted files emptied from the Windows Recycle Bin, or files lost due to the format or corruption of a hard drive, virus or Trojan infection, unexpected system shutdown, or software failure.

The following are some of the features of Recover My Files:

- Recover from hard drive, camera card, USB, Zip, floppy disk, iPod, and other media
- Recover files even if **emptied from the Recycle Bin**
- File recovery after **accidental format**, even if you have **reinstalled Windows**
- Disk recovery after a **hard disk crash**
- Get back files after a **partitioning error**
- Get data back from **RAW hard drives**
- Recover documents, photos, video music, and e-mail
- Recovers NTFS, FAT(12/16/32), exFAT, HFS, HFS+

Tool: Undelete

Operating Systems: Windows NT 4.0 Workstation, 2000 Professional, XP Home Edition, XP Professional Edition, Vista, and Windows 7, as well as Windows Server 2000, 2003, and 2008
File Types: All
Media: Hard drives, including RAID arrays, and removable media
Web Site: *http://www.condusiv.com/products/undelete/*
Cost: $59.95

The following are some of the features of Undelete:

- Enables easy recovery of deleted and overwritten local and network files
- Provides continuous data protection for Windows PCs and servers
- Recovers previous or overwritten versions of Word, Excel, and PowerPoint files
- Allows self-service recovery, relieving IT from this task
- Instantly recovers files in virtual environments
- Central management through Undelete Server

4

Tool: VirtualLab

Operating Systems: Windows, Mac OS 9.x and X
File Types: All
Media: Hard drives and removable media
Web Site: *http://www.condusiv.com/products/undelete/*
Cost: $59.00 GBP Basic; $109.00 GBP Professional

VirtualLab recovers deleted files from removable drive formats and digital camera media. It recovers files from disks no longer recognized by the operating system. The VirtualLab application also undeletes files thrown in the trash or deleted by a virus. It recovers deleted files and ghosted or damaged partitions. The program also recovers files after a format or restore from original system disks. It recovers damaged RAID servers and failed rebuilds. The X1 application quickly locates e-mails, files on the hard disk, and Web pages.

- *Volume Recover*: From formatted drives, or disks that won't mount, Volume Recover will perform an exhaustive scan, find data, and show the results in a Mac-like Finder interface.
- *RAID Reconstructor*: VirtualLab Mac OS X now has a RAID reconstructor.
- *Undelete*: Recovers deleted files quickly, even those hidden from the operating system.
- *Photos*: VirtualLab supports all camera card formats and can recover lost photos not saved on a computer using an iPhoto-like browser.
- *Firewire/USB*: VirtualLab recognizes all Firewire and USB external or portable drives. Simply connect the drive to a Mac and click **Scan**. VirtualLab will display all the disks it can recover.
- *Universal Support*: Mac OS X version runs on Intel-based Macs. Also, VirtualLab Mac OS X will recover older OS 9 (Classic) volumes. The Windows version will recover Mac and Windows-formatted disks.

Tools for Use with UNIX-Based Systems

Tool: e2undel

Operating Systems: Linux ext2 only
Web Site: *http://e2undel.sourceforge.net/*
Cost: Free

The e2undel tool supports Linux systems with the ext2 file system. It includes a library that can recover deleted files by the file name.

Ext2 is an old UNIX file system. When a file is recovered in a medium, three parts of the file should be checked: file content; metadata that contains creation time, date, owner and user rights of the file; and the file name. This tool does not manipulate the internal ext2 structure. It requires only read access to the file system.

This tool is not compatible with other Linux file systems, such as ext3, ReiserFS, XFS, and JFS.

Tool: R-Linux

Operating Systems: Recovers Linux ext2 file system; Host OS: Windows 9*x*, ME, NT, 2000, XP, Vista, 7, 8
File Types: All
Media: Logical and physical disks, including network drives and removable media
Web Site: *http://www.r-tt.com/*
Cost: Free

R-Linux is a free data recovery tool that supports the ext2 file system in Linux and other UNIX versions. Files from logical disks are recovered, even if the records are lost. It creates image files for the entire disk/partition, or for a part of it. Such image files can be processed like regular disks. The application recognizes localized names. R-Linux can also recover files that can be saved on any disks accessible by the host operating system.

R-Linux uses a unique IntelligentScan technology and a flexible parameter setting that gives the investigator control over the data recovery. It recovers files from existing logical disks even when file records are lost. R-Linux is a "lite" version of a more powerful file recover utility, R-Studio. R-Studio utilizes the IntelligentScan technology to its full extent, and can recover data from partitions with broken file systems. Also, R-Studio can recover data over a network.

The following are some of the features of R-Linux:

- Standard Windows Explorer–style interface
- Can save recovered files on any disks visible to the host operating system
- Recovers files from disks with bad sectors

Tool: OfficeFIX Platinum Professional

Operating Systems: Windows and Mac OS
File Types: Microsoft Office files only
Media: N/A
Web Site: *http://www.cimaware.com/*
Cost: $279.00

4

OfficeFIX is a Microsoft Office recovery suite. OfficeFIX recovers the information from a damaged or corrupted file, and stores it into a new file. It includes data recovery from ExcelFIX, AccesssFIX, OutlookFIX, and WordFIX.

The following are some of the features of OfficeFIX:

- It recovers data from MS Access 2013, 2010, 2007, 2003, 2002 (XP), 2000, 97, and 95.
- It supports all versions of MS Excel.
- It also recovers data from all versions of MS Word documents, including Word for Macintosh.

The following are some of the limitations of OfficeFIX:

- It does not recover Excel sheets with:
  - Password-protected files
  - Visual Basic and macros
  - Array formulas
  - Pivot tables (only cell values are recovered)
- It does not recover password-protected access files if the **security file** option is set.
- It does not recover password-protected Word files.
- It recovers text data, table data, and basic formatting in a document.
- It does not recover Japanese or Chinese characters.
- WordFIX cannot currently repair embedded OLE objects in Word documents, such as Excel spreadsheets and Microsoft Visio diagrams, or audio or video files, ActiveX controls, or macros.

Tool: Zip Repair Pro

Operating Systems: Windows
File Types: Compressed files (.zip)
Media: N/A
Web Site: *http://www.ziprepair.com/*
Cost: $29.95

Zip Repair Pro is a utility that will repair corrupt Zip files. Usually a corrupt Zip file gives the error message:

"Cannot open file: it does not appear to be a valid archive."

The following are some of the features of Zip Repair Pro:

- Creates an error-free backup of a user's original file for instant access
- Fixes CRC errors in .zip files so that data can still be uncompressed
- Supports spanned Zip volumes, including the Zip64 format; a user can now repair and extract from a spanned Zip set, even if part of the set is missing.
- Supports huge file sizes 2 GB+ (as long as there is enough disk space)

Type

Tool: CD Data Rescue

Operating Systems: Windows
File Types: All
Media: CDs and DVDs
Web Site: *http://www.naltech.com/cddr.htm*
Cost: $19.95

CD Data Rescue recovers files from damaged, scratched, or defective CD-ROM, CD-R, and CD-RW discs. It also supports Mount Rainier/Easy Write (MRW) discs. With this product, a user can easily recover files, folders, or deleted files from CDs. It also can recover files from quick-formatted CD-RW discs.

CD Data Rescue recovers unreadable and deleted files from CDs recorded by common CD writing software in ISO and UDF formats. It features full real UDF recovery supported for UDF packet-writing software (mode B): DirectCD (including old versions and compressed CDs), InCD, packetCD, and so on. The tool also supports discs recorded by Sony digital cameras.

The following are some of the features of CD Data Rescue:

- Updated Recovery Wizard
- Automatically detects and renames unnamed files with the correct file type
- Complete UDF file system recovery
- Uses exclusive recovery technology that allows a user to achieve the best performance recovering data
- Can recover data from CDs and DVDs recorded in the ISO 9660 format and UDF format

Tool: DiskInternals Flash Recovery

Operating Systems: Windows 95, 98, ME, NT, 2000, XP, and 2003 Server
File Types: All
Media: Flash memory devices
Web Site: *http://www.diskinternals.com/flash-recovery/features.shtml*
Cost: $39.95

DiskInternals Flash Recovery is a flash memory file recovery tool that restores corrupted and deleted photographs, or ones lost due to hardware malfunctions. This utility works even if a memory card was reformatted. The program recovers images from hard drives, external drives, cameras, and flash memory devices such as SmartMedia, CompactFlash, Memory Stick, MicroDrive, xD Picture Card, Flash Card, PC Card, Multimedia Card, Secure Digital Card, and many others.

The following are some of the features of DiskInternals Flash Recovery:

- Easy Recovery Wizard
- Can preview and recover JPEG, JPG, TIFF, BMP, PNG, GIF, TGA, and other images
- Supports FAT12, FAT16, FAT32, NTFS (NT 4), NTFS5 (2000, XP), UDF, ISO 9660, ext2/3, HPFS
- Can save recovered files on any (including network) disks visible to the host operating system
- Creates recovery snapshot files for logical drives; these files can be processed like regular disks.
- Recovers pictures deleted by accident
- Recovers photos from erased or formatted media or deleted from digital cameras or the Recycle Bin
- Allows a user to preview recoverable images before purchasing the program

Tool: IsoBuster

Operating Systems: Windows (but works on Mac-formatted discs)
File Types: All
Media: CD, DVD, and Blu-ray formats (BD and HD DVDs)
Web Site: *http://www.isobuster.com/isobuster.php*
Cost: $39.95

IsoBuster is a highly specialized, yet easy-to-use CD, DVD, and Blu-ray data recovery tool. It supports all CD, DVD, and Blu-ray formats (BD and HD DVDs) and common CD, DVD, and Blu-ray file systems. Start up IsoBuster, insert a disk, select the drive (if not selected already), and let IsoBuster compile the media. IsoBuster immediately shows the user all the tracks and sessions located on the media, combined with all file systems that are present. This way, the user gets access to all the files and folders per file system instead of being limited to one file system. The user can access data from older sessions and data that Windows does not see or hides from view.

The following are some of the features of IsoBuster:

- Recovers data from all possible CD, DVD, and Blu-ray formats: CD-i, VCD, SVCD, SACD, CD-ROM, CD-ROM XA, CD-R, CD-RW, CD-MRW, DVD-ROM, DVCD, DVD-RAM, DVD-R, DVD-RW, DVD+R, DVD+RW, DVD+MRW, DVD+R Dual Layer, DVD-R Dual Layer, DVD+RW Dual Layer, DVD+VR, DVD+VRW, DVD-VR, DVD-VRW, DVD-VM, DVD-VFR, BD-ROM, BD-R, BD-R DL, BD-RE, BD-RE DL, BD-R SRM, BD-R RRM, BD-R SRM+POW, BD-R SRM-POW, BDAV, BDMV HD DVD-ROM, HD DVD-R, HD DVD-R DL, HD DVD-RW, HD DVD-RW DL, HD DVD-RAM, HD DVD-Video, …

- Exclusively provides all device access, media access, data gathering, and interpretation; it does not rely on Windows to provide or interpret the data, and so can work completely independently from Windows' limitations.

- Uses primary and secondary file systems to get to the data and/or make use of file system data that might be ignored or forgotten by the operating system

- Supports mounting several virtual sessions inside a single DVD+RW or DVD-RW track

- Reads and extracts files, CD/DVD images, tracks, and sessions from all optical media

- Scans for lost UDF files and folders, and for lost ISO 9660/Joliet sessions

- Finds lost data on CDs or DVDs created with integrated drag-and-drop applications, otherwise known as packet-writing software; optimized, but not exclusively, for Roxio Direct CD, Roxio Drag-to-Disc, Ahead/Nero InCD, Prassi/Veritas/Sonic DLA, VOB/Pinnacle Instant-Write, and CeQuadrat Packet CD

- Supports direct CD compressed files

- Built-in UDF reader, UDF 1.02 (e.g., DVDs), UDF 1.5 (e.g., packet writing on CD-R, DVD+R, DVD-R, CD-RW, DVD+RW, and DVD-RW), and UDF 2.01, 2.50

- Finds lost pictures created and saved to CD or DVD with Sony Mavica, other digital cameras, or other devices with embedded UDF write functionality

- Finds lost movies created and saved to CD or DVD with Hitachi, other digital cameras, or other devices with embedded UDF write functionality

- Automatically finds extensions based on file content to try to give an appropriate name to an orphaned file; this built-in file identifier assigns the proper extension to the file so that Windows applications can open the file. Only needed for orphaned files without a name.

- Has transparent built-in support for Mac Resource Fork extensions in the UDF file system

Recovering Deleted Partitions

Deletion of a Partition

In Windows systems, a user can delete a partition by:

- Using the Windows interface
- Using a command line

What Happens When a Partition Is Deleted?

- When a user deletes a partition on any logical drive, all the data on that drive is lost.
- If a user deletes a partition on a dynamic disk, all dynamic volumes on the disk are deleted, thus corrupting the disk.

Deletion of a Partition Using the Windows Interface Use the following procedure to delete a partition using the Windows interface:

- Open Computer Management:
    - Click **Start** → **Control Panel**.
    - Double-click **Administrative Tools** → **Computer Management**.

- In the console tree:
  - Click **Computer Management (Local)** → **Storage** → **Disk Management.**
- Right-click the partition, logical drive, or basic volume you want to delete, and then click **Delete Partition**.

Figure 4-1 shows deletion of a partition using Computer Management.

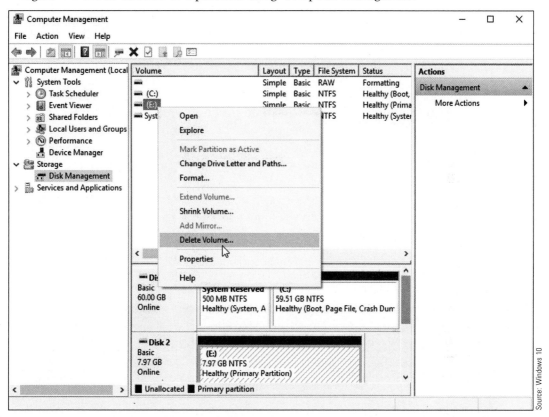

Figure 4-1   Deletion of a partition using the Computer Management utility.

Deletion of a Partition Using the Command Line Use the following steps to delete a partition using the command line:

- At the command prompt, type **diskpart.**
- At the DiskPart prompt:
  - Type **list disk:**
    - Note the disk number of the disk from which the partition is to be deleted.
- Type **select disk n:**
  - Selects disk number *n.*
- Type **list partition:**
  - Note the number of partitions.
- Type **select partition n:**
  - Selects partition *n.*

Common Terms

List disk: It gives the list of disks and information about each disk, such as its size, free space available, whether the disk is basic or dynamic, and if the disk uses either a master boot record (MBR) or GUID partition table (GPT) partition.

Select disk: It selects the specified disk; *n* denotes the disk number.

List partition: It shows the list of partitions in the partition table of the current disk.

Select partition: It selects the specified partition *n* that denotes the partition number. If the partition is not provided, the select command lists the current partition.

Delete partition: It deletes the partition. Partitions such as a system partition or boot partition, which contains an active paging file or crash dump, cannot be deleted.

- Type **delete partition:**
  - Deletes the partition.

Figures 4-2, 4-3, and 4-4 show screenshots from DiskPart.

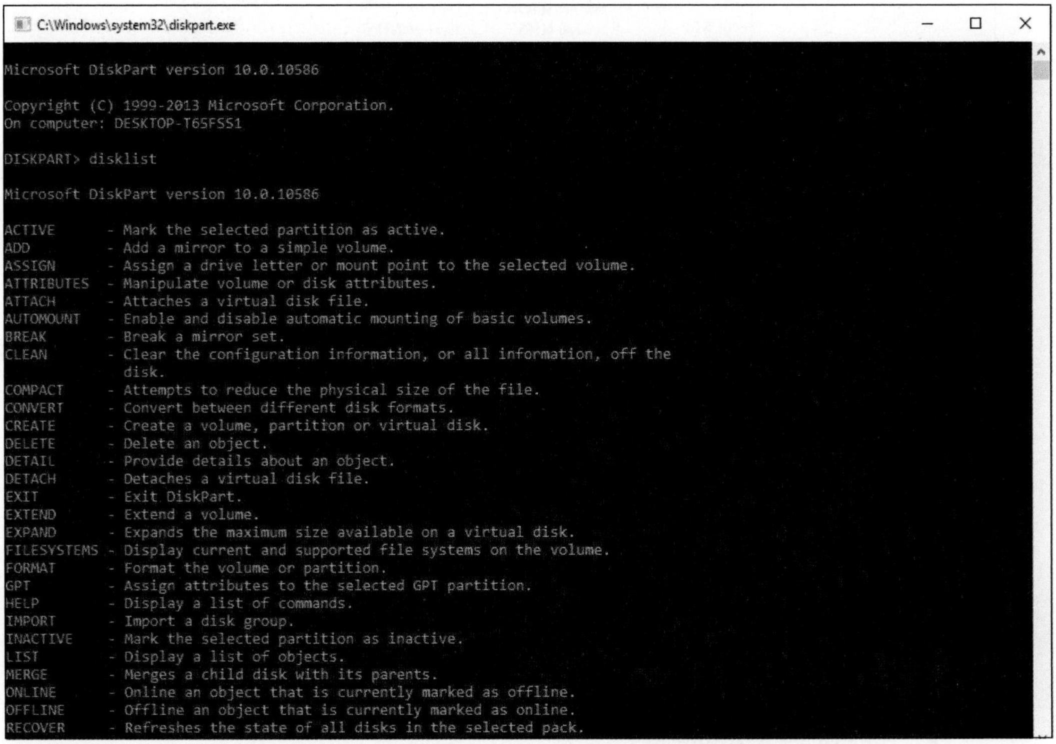

Figure 4-2 The available switches that can be used with the DiskPart command.

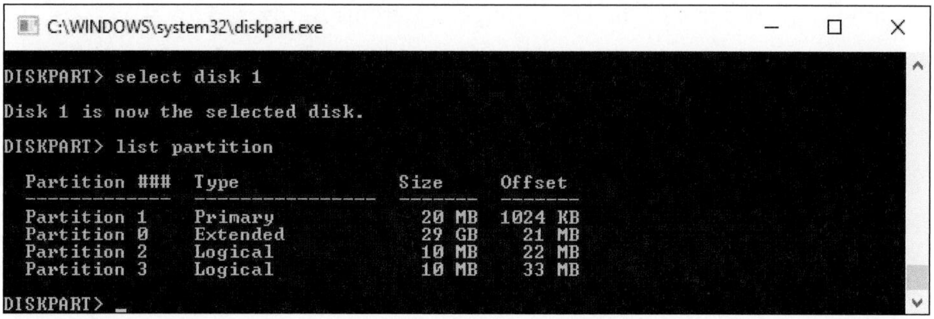

Source: Windows 10

Figure 4-3 Notice the four different partitions. Different partitions can have different types, such as Primary or Extended, with logical drives being part of the extended partition.

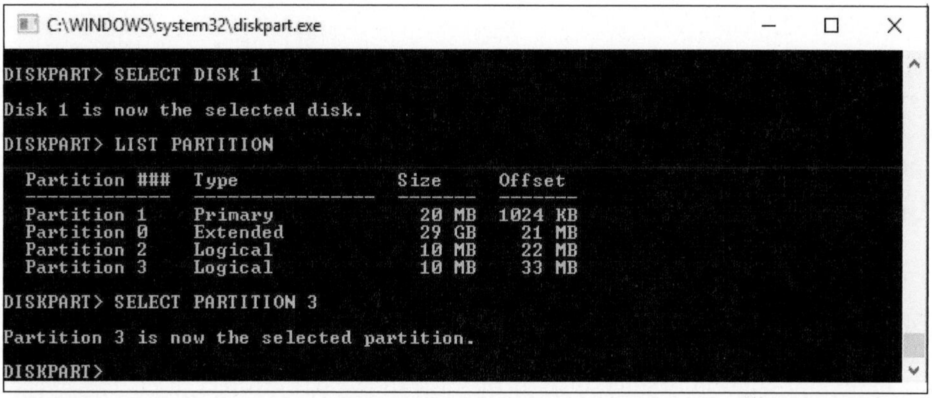

Source: Windows 10

Figure 4-4 The command Delete Partition will remove the information from partition 3. The data will still be stored, but it will be unavailable to the user, as the space will be listed in the OS as free space and may be overwritten as new information is stored.

Recovery of Deleted Partitions

The recovery of deleted partitions is the process by which a user can evaluate and extract deleted partitions. The partition recovery process is important in case of data recovery. This recovery helps in recovering the partitions that are lost accidentally, or due to virus, software malfunction, or even sabotage. There are some tools available for the recovery of deleted partitions.

Tools to Recover Deleted and Damaged Partitions

Tool: Acronis Recovery Expert Acronis Recovery Expert, included in the Acronis Disk Director Suite 10.0, completely protects a user's data, allowing him or her to recover deleted or lost partitions. It also protects the user's system from hardware or software failure, virus attack, or hacker intrusion.

If a user's PC becomes unbootable after a power outage or a system error, he or she can recover it with Acronis Recovery Expert.

The following are some of the key features of Acronis Recovery Expert:

- Supports the following file systems: FAT16, FAT32, NTFS, HPFS (OS/2); ext2, ext3, ReiserFS, Swap (Linux)
- Provides automatic and manual recovery modes
- Independently works from bootable CDs or diskettes, enabling a user to recover partitions even if his or her operating system fails to boot
- Supports large disks over 180 GB
- Provides a Windows XP–like wizard-style interface for superior usability and ease of use

Tool: Active@ Disk Image   Active@ Disk Image is a DOS-based solution designed for complete backup and restoration of the whole HDD, as well as the particular FAT/NTFS partitions and logical drives.

Users can create compressed and noncompressed raw images (containing all of a drive's data—a mirror of a drive's surface stored in one or a set of files), as well as compressed data images (containing only the drive's used clusters, saving users space and increasing speed).

A unique feature of Active@ Disk Image is the ability to open disk images and preview files and folders inside, before image restoration. Users can even copy specific files or folders from the image to another location.

To restore accidentally deleted files, use Active@ Disk Image to make an image of the disk (snapshot), from which users can later try to restore deleted files without the risk of overwriting important data on original disk. If the disk shows bad clusters, users can effectively stop this process to preserve whatever is still readable as an image, and try to restore data later.

The following are some of the features of Active@ Disk Image:

- Can be run from a DOS bootable floppy or CD-ROM
- Displays complete HDD, partition, and disk image information
- Creates compressed and noncompressed raw images for the physical drive (HDD)
- Restores compressed and noncompressed raw images back to the physical drive or partition
- Creates compressed data images for any partition on the HDD
- Displays contents of any physical sector on the drive or within the disk image
- Allows viewing of all files and folders inside disk image before restoration using the preview mode
- Allows the copying of specific files and folders from the image to another location
- Supports IDE/ATA/SCSI/USB drives
- Supports large (more than 128 GB) hard disk drives and partitions
- Supports FAT12, FAT16, FAT32, NTFS, and NTFS5 file systems
- Supports partitions created in MS-DOS, Windows 95/98/ME/NT/2000/XP/2003/XP Professional x64/XP/7 and 8 Home x64/2003/2003,2008/2012 Server x64

Tool: Active@ Partition Recovery Active@ Partition Recovery for DOS can recover deleted partitions only if its location on a hard disk drive has not already been overwritten. If an MBR backup was created by using Active@ Partition Recovery, users can always restore MBR and partition information.

Active@ Partition Recovery for Windows will help if a nonsystem partition is lost (i.e., users can boot Windows, install, and run the software from under the Windows operating system to recover deleted or damaged partitions located on data volumes). BOOT.INI is corrected automatically (if needed) to keep the system bootable, and damaged volume boot sectors are corrected to maintain integrity of the partition. The software can repair the MBR and delete invalid partitions.

Active@ Partition Recovery can:

- Recover deleted partitions (FAT, FAT32, and NTFS)
- Restore deleted FAT and NTFS logical drives
- Create drive images for backup purposes
- Scan hard drives and detect deleted FAT and NTFS partitions and/or logical drives
- Preview files and folders on deleted partition or drive, to recover proper data
- Backup MBR, partition table, and boot sectors
- Restore MBRs, partition tables, and boot sectors from backup if damaged
- Undelete partitions (primary and extended)
- Be stored on a bootable floppy disk due to its small size
- Display complete physical and logical drive information
- Be used with ease: controlled by only arrow, Enter, and Esc keys

Tool: DiskInternals Partition Recovery DiskInternals Partition Recovery is intended for users who need to recover data or lost partitions. DiskInternals Partition Recovery includes a step-by-step wizard and requires no special skills to operate. This product includes DiskInternals NTFS and DiskInternals FAT recovery products.

DiskInternals Partition Recovery recovers data from damaged, deleted, lost, or reformatted partitions, image files, or important documents. The software includes a Partition Recovery Wizard, NTFS Recovery Wizard, and a FAT Recovery Wizard.

DiskInternals Partition Recovery supports a multitude of file systems, including:

- FAT12, FAT16, FAT32, and VFAT
- NTFS, NTFS4, and NTFS5
- ext2, ext3

The tool scans every disk sector for recoverable data. DiskInternals Partition Recovery repairs data from virtual disks, and it does not matter if these files or folders were deleted before recovery or not.

Tool: Partition Table Doctor The Partition Table Doctor will recover a user's data if the partition table, or boot sector, on a hard disk is lost or damaged due to a virus attack, software failure, Fdisk or PartitionMagic misapplication, and so on. The Partition Table Doctor can recover partitions.

The Partition Table Doctor only modifies a partition table or boot sector, which means that the software will never attempt to write to the data area of the drive that a user wants to recover.

Partition Recovery tools provide a graphical user interface (GUI), and it is easy to create an emergency floppy disk or bootable CD. Though the software is easy to follow, advanced users can improve the results by analyzing the reports, examining the file system details, and selecting specific sectors to modify.

Tool: Scaven   Scaven is a microtool for data recovery. It was designed to perform unattended multisession searches through large hard drives. It records the position of matches found to the output text file in a sector: offset: match format (fixed size column).

Scaven is an effective tool and time saver in recovering data from:

- Files permanently deleted
- Files lost through overwrite
- Accidentally formatted drives
- Drives with damaged MBR/lost partitions
- Drives with corrupted FATs
- Drives that have developed bad sectors

The following are some of the features of Scaven:

- Performs a multiple-string search in a single pass
- Works with any size LBA hard drive (up to 138 GB)
- Automatically detects drive geometry (CHS and LBA)
- Can access drives invisible on DOS
- Fits on a single floppy and leaves plenty of room (size <10k) on the hard drive
- Records the position of matches found as sector number: offset
- Records the location of bad sectors as a sector number
- Uses standard text files for input/output
- Was written in a plain assembler for the sake of size/speed

Tool: TestDisk   TestDisk is free data-recovery software. It was primarily designed to help recover lost partitions and/or make nonbooting disks bootable when these symptoms are caused by faulty software, certain types of viruses, or human error (such as accidentally deleting the partition table).

TestDisk supports the following operating systems:

- DOS (either *real* or in a Windows 9x DOS-box)
- Windows NT4, 2000, XP, 2003, Vista, 2008, Windows 7 (x86, x64)
- Linux

- FreeBSD, NetBSD, OpenBSD
- SunOS
- Mac OS X

TestDisk can find lost partitions for the following file systems:

- BeFS (BeOS)
- BSD disklabel (FreeBSD/OpenBSD/Net BSD)
- CramFS, Compressed File System
- DOS/Windows FAT12, FAT16, and FAT32
- HFS and HFS+
- JFS, IBM's Journaled File System
- Linux ext2 and ext3
- Linux Raid

4

TestDisk queries the BIOS or the OS in order to find the hard disks and their characteristics (LBA size and CHS geometry). TestDisk does a quick check of the user's disk's structure, and compares it with the user's partition table for entry errors. If the partition table has entry errors, TestDisk can repair them. If the user has missing partitions, or a completely empty partition table, TestDisk can search for partitions and create a new table, or even a new MBR, if necessary.

However, it is up to the user to look over the list of possible partitions found by TestDisk and to select the one(s) that were being used just before the drive failed to boot or the partition(s) were lost. In some cases, especially after initiating a detailed search for lost partitions, TestDisk may show partition data that is simply the remnants of a partition that had been deleted and overwritten long ago.

TestDisk has features for both novices and experts. For those who know little or nothing about data recovery techniques, TestDisk can be used to collect detailed information about a nonbooting drive, which can then be sent to a tech for further analysis. Those more familiar with such procedures should find TestDisk a handy tool in performing on-site recovery.

Chapter Summary

- In Windows, files in the Recycle Bin are stored in the C:\RECYCLED folder on FAT file systems, and in the C:\RECYCLER folder on NTFS file systems.
- Files or folders deleted from removable media are not stored in the Recycle Bin.
- Damaged files in the Recycled folder do not appear in the Recycle Bin.
- In Linux, files that are deleted using /bin/rm remain on the disk.
- Deleting a partition on a dynamic disk can delete all dynamic volumes on the disk, thus leaving the disk in a corrupt state.
- Recovery of deleted partitions is the process by which the investigator evaluates and extracts deleted partitions.

Key Terms

Recycle Bin   security identifier (SID)
recycled folder   undelete

Review Questions

1. What happens when a file is deleted in Windows?

   _____

   _____

   _____

   _____

2. How does the Recycle Bin work in Windows?

   _____

   _____

   _____

   _____

3. Why are the Recycle Bin folders differently named on NTFS and FAT file systems?

   _____

   _____

   _____

   _____

4. Explain the following:

   a. Damaged or deleted INFO2 file

   b. Damaged Recycled folder

   _____

   _____

   _____

   _____

5. Describe the data recovery process in Linux.

_____

_____

_____

_____

6. How can you delete a partition using the command line?

_____

_____

_____

_____

7. Write down the steps to delete a partition using the Windows interface.

_____

_____

_____

_____

8. Which tools recover deleted files in Linux?

_____

_____

_____

_____

9. Which tool would you use to recover lost partitions? Why?

_____

_____

_____

_____

Hands-On Projects

1. Use Recover My Files to recover deleted files:
   - Using your preferred Internet browser, navigate to *http://www.recovermyfiles.com/* to download and install the latest version of Recover My Files.
   - Launch Recover My Files.
   - Select the **"Recover Files"** option and click **"Next"**.
 - Select the drive you want to recover files from and click **"Next"**.
 - Select **"Search for deleted files"** and click **"Start"**.
 - Once the search is complete, expand the drive in the left pane.
 - Change to the different Recovery views to see the grouping options results displayed in the right pane (Figure 4-5).

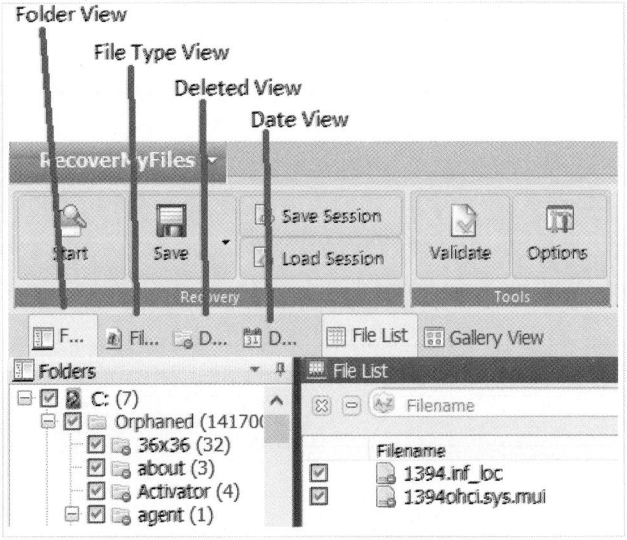

Figure 4-5   Recovery views in Recover My Files.

 - Prepare a one-paragraph summary of your efforts and the benefits of this tool in a forensic investigation.

2. Use EaseUS Partition Recovery Wizard to recover a deleted partition:
   - Using your preferred Internet browser, navigate to *http://www.ptdd.com/windows-data-recovery/partition-recovery-software.html* to download and install the latest version of EaseUS Partition Recovery Wizard.
   - Launch EaseUS Partition Recovery Wizard.
   - Select **"Partition Recovery"**.
   - This screen identifies the disks attached to the current system. Select a disk to search for deleted partitions on and click **"Next"**.
   - Select **"Search Entire Disk"** and click **"Next"**.
   - Select **"Fast"** and click **"Next"**.

- This screen shows partitions available for recovery. **DO NOT PROCEED!** (Unless you are on a test system that you do not care about corrupting).
- Click "**Quit**" at this point (Figure 4-6).

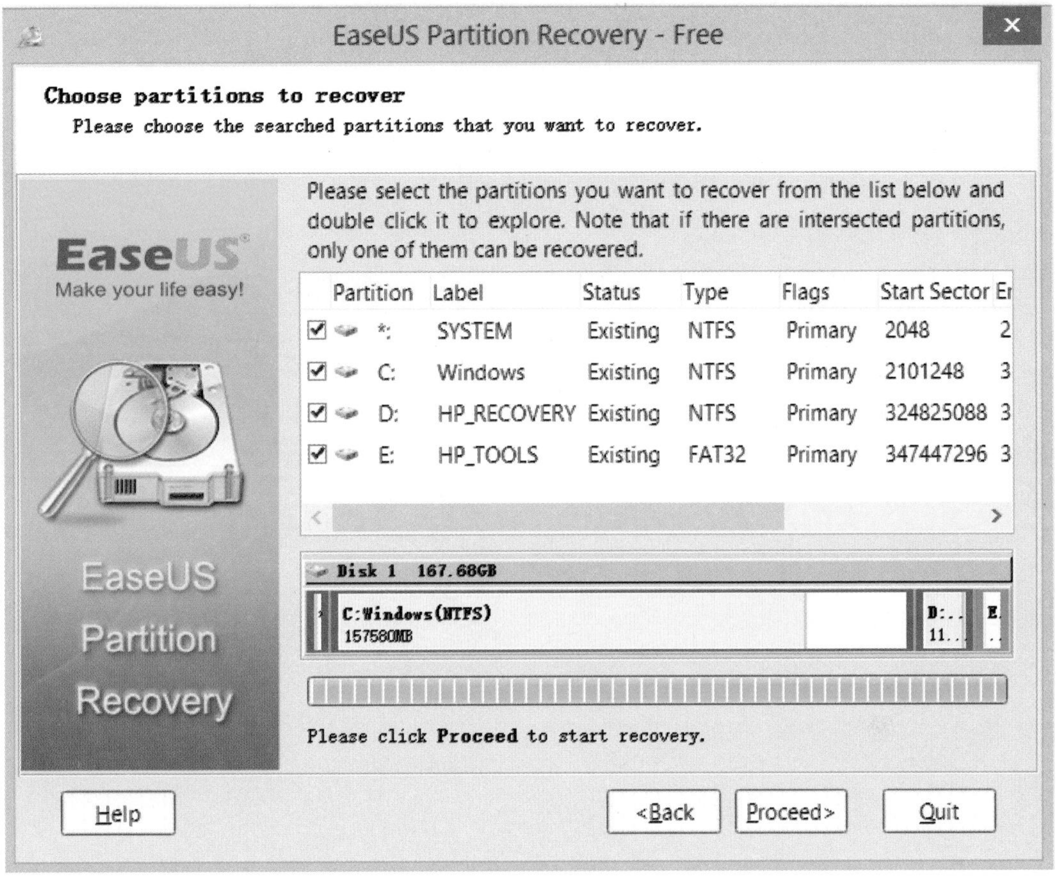

Source: EaseUS Partition Recovery

Figure 4-6 Partitions available for recovery in EaseUS Partition Recovery Free Edition.

- Prepare a one-paragraph summary of the benefits of this tool in a forensic investigation.

3. Review file recovery tools:
   - Pick three file recovery tools mentioned in this chapter, and one file recovery tool not mentioned, to review.
   - Identify and compare the features of each tool. In addition to the obvious features such as cost, operating system compatibility, pros, or cons, also comment on end-user features such as effort to locate, ease-of-use, and so on. Identify no less than 10 comparison points.
   - Prepare a table detailing the results of your research.

chapter 5

Image File Forensics

After completing this chapter, you should be able to:

- Recognize graphic image files
- Explain data compression
- Locate and recover graphic image files
- Analyze graphic image file headers
- Reconstruct file fragments
- Identify and use tools for viewing graphic images
- Understand steganography in graphic image files
- Perform steganalysis in graphic image files
- Identify and use graphic image file forensic tools

What If?

Assistant Attorney General Alice S. Fisher, of the Criminal Division, and U.S. Attorney Chuck Rosenberg, of the Eastern District of Virginia, announced in Federal Court on September 8, 2006, the sentencing of Nathan L. Peterson, of Antelope Acres, California, to 87 months imprisonment.

Peterson was accused of stealing intellectual property of various software companies, such as Adobe Systems Inc., Macromedia Inc., Microsoft Corporation, Sonic Solutions, and Symantec Corporation. Peterson ran a Web site, *http://www.ibackups.net*, and sold illegal copies of copyrighted software products at a price lower than the suggested retail price. The software was reproduced and distributed through an instantaneous computer download of an electronic copy, and/or by shipment through the mail on CDs.

As of February 2005, Peterson had made illegal sales of over $5.4 million of copyrighted software, which resulted in a loss of approximately $20 million to the owners. With this money, Peterson led a lavish lifestyle that included multiple homes and a boat. He also maintained numerous assets, such as bank accounts and a garage full of stylish cars.

After receiving complaints from copyright holders, an FBI undercover agent, posing as a customer, made purchases from the Web site. As a result of this investigation, the Web site was discontinued in February 2005. On December 13 of the same year, Peterson pleaded guilty to two counts of criminal copyright infringement for selling pirated software. The court also forfeited the proceeds of his illegal conduct and ordered him to pay restitution of more than $5.4 million.

- How did the FBI determine that the software was pirated from the original vendors?
- How was metadata imbedded into the images of the software companies to prevent copyright violations?

Introduction to Image File Forensics

This chapter covers the various methods in which a forensic investigator can go about recovering graphics files. This chapter mainly deals with understanding the basic concept of recovering graphics files. The chapter also highlights the various image recovery, steganalysis, and viewing tools that are used and the salient features of these tools.

Introduction to Image Files

An image is an artifact that reproduces the likeness of some object. Photographs, faxes, photocopies, reflections, and views from microscopes and telescopes are all images. Computer forensics, with regard to recovering graphic image files, is of prime importance to many corporate organizations. A large number of computer forensics investigations include graphic images, typically downloaded from the Internet and sent through e-mails by employees of the company. In order to examine and recover these deleted files, a computer investigator needs to know the basics of image file graphics, including:

- Features of graphic image files
- Common image file formats
- Compression methods used by image files

Computer forensic investigators need to identify image file fragments and repair damaged image file headers. There are many tools in a computer forensic investigator's arsenal to recover image files. Examiners also give importance to the process of steganography, in which data is hidden inside files and images. They also analyze image file headers from unknown image file formats, a painstaking process. It is important to properly recover image files in order to use the hidden data as evidence.

There are four different kinds that can be used in an image. The **CMYK** scale is best for print production. The colors used in a CMYK image are percentages of cyan (blue), magenta (reddish-pink), yellow, and black. These result in millions of possible color combinations. Another scale is **RGB** (red, green, blue), which results in 256 possible colors. **Indexed color** contains the colors in RGB, but only the colors used by the image. Images can also be **gray-scale**, which only shows shades of the colors black and white.

There are several different kinds of image file formats. Image formats can differ in color, ease of use, and size during the reproduction process. They also have specific internal structures that are important to an investigator analyzing or repairing files.

Images can be broadly categorized into vector images and raster images.

Understanding Vector Images

Vector images use geometrical shapes and primitives, such as points, lines, curves, and polygons, based upon mathematical equations, in order to represent images in a computer. Because each image is basically an equation, it is easy to move, scale, rotate, and fill a completed image. The file size of a vector image is relatively small, because it stores only the mathematical calculations, not the images, of the pictures included. Vector images can be easily embedded into another program without bloating the host file size.

It is possible to enlarge a vector image without affecting the quality of the image; the graphic program simply multiplies the existing pixels on the image file by the magnification you select. When investigators examine images in forensic investigations, they can enlarge elements greatly to examine them better.

Vector files can be converted into raster files, as long as there are no other images, such as digital photography or scanned photographs, in the vector file format.

Understanding Raster Images

Unlike vector images, **raster images** are composed of a collection of pixels. A **pixel** is a single point in a graphic image. The quality of raster images is specified by the number of pixels present and information present in each pixel. Because the number of pixels is fixed when the image is set, if you enlarge the image, it loses its quality. (Imagine a photograph. When you enlarge the photograph, the picture becomes blurry, and it is harder to see specific elements.)

In every raster image, pixels are associated with three 8-bit color values (0–255 values) that define the amount of each of the three colors (red, green, and blue) in each pixel. Images that have less color require less information per pixel. Images that have only black and white pixels contain only a single bit for each piece of information.

File formats such as BMP, JPEG, and GIF are examples of the raster image. In a raster image, the pixels are arranged in rows that make the image file easier to print. When any type of image is printed, it has to be converted to a raster image first to print the pixels line by line, in order to finish the complete set of pixels.

Metafile Graphics Metafile graphics include both raster and vector images. When a metafile is enlarged, some parts of the image show a lower resolution, thereby giving the image a shady appearance. An example of a metafile is a photograph of an image file with arrows superimposed on the photograph. If a metafile is enlarged, the area created with a raster format loses some resolution, and the quality of the file will be low. However, the formatted area of the vector will remain sharp and clear without any loss to compression.

Understanding Image File Formats

A file format is a way to encode information to be stored in a computer file. Graphical editors that can save image file formats include Microsoft Paint, Macromedia Freehand, Adobe Photoshop, and GIMP for Linux. Many of these graphic editors are especially optimized for one particular file format. For example, Microsoft Paint can be used to work on only bitmap images. Macromedia Freehand generates and reads vector shapes. Forensic investigators usually use Adobe Photoshop, as it works on both bitmap images as well as vector graphics.

Many graphic-editing applications allow the examiner to create and save files in one or more of the standard image file formats. Table 5-1 shows commonly used image file formats.

File Format	File Extension
Graphics Interchange Format (GIF)	.gif
Joint Photographic Experts Group (JPEG)	.jpg
Tagged Image File Format (TIFF)	.tif
Windows Bitmap (BMP)	.bmp
JPEG 2000	.jp2
Portable Network Graphics (PNG)	.png

Table 5-1   Popular standard image formats and file extensions

GIF (Graphics Interchange Format) GIF is a file format that contains 8 bits per pixel and displays 256 colors per frame. CompuServe generated the GIF format in 1987. GIF uses lossless data compression techniques, which maintain the visual quality of the image.

Features of GIF are as follows:

- *Limited color palette*: GIF image file consists of a color table, which stores the image consisting of 2, 4, 8, 16, 32, 64, 128, or 256 colors. Each color in this table contains an RGB (Red, Green, Blue) value within a range of zero to 255. GIF does not support the CMYK (Cyan, Magenta, Yellow, Key [Black]) color combination.

- *Dithering*: The size of the GIF file depends on the number of colors used. For example, if 256 colors are used, then it becomes 9.5 Kb. For 32 colors, it becomes 4.4 Kb, and for 16 colors, it is 1.9 Kb. **Dithering** is used to limit the size file. It combines smaller color dots together to form greater color depth. Dithering adds noise to the image and it decreases the sharpness of the image.

- *LZW compression*: GIF uses the LZW (Lempel-Ziv-Welch) compression technique. This lossless data compression algorithm combines the string of same byte values into the single code word. It reduces the size of the 8-bit pixel data by about 40 percent or greater.

- *Interlacing*: GIF has a Web-specific feature known as **interlacing**. It helps to display the image quickly on the screen. This feature first shows the low-resolution version of the image and gradually displays the full version of the image.

GIF File Structure A GIF file, consists of the following elements:

- *Header*: The GIF file starts with a 6-byte header, which identifies the type of GIF image. The first three bytes identify the file as the GIF format. The second three bytes tell the version of GIF format: 87a or 89a.

```
typedef struct _GifHeader
{
// Header
BYTE Signature[3]; /* Header Signature (always "GIF") */
BYTE Version[3]; /* GIF format version ("87a" or "89a") */
}
```

- *Logical screen descriptor*: The logical screen descriptor contains data about the screen and color, which helps to display the GIF image. It describes the ScreenHeight and ScreenWidth fields, as well as screen resolution.

- *Global color table*: The logical screen descriptor is followed by the global color table. The size of the table depends upon the number of colors chosen for the image. All GIF images include three colors: red, green, and blue. There are 256 possible combinations of these three colors that can create a spectrum of colors accessible to the user. When saving an image, the user selects a maximum amount of colors in the final image, always in the power of two (i.e., 2, 4, 8, 16, 32, . . . 256). The more colors selected, the larger the file.

```
typedef struct _GifColorTable
{
BYTE Red; /* Red Color Element */
BYTE Green; /* Green Color Element */
BYTE Blue; /* Blue Color Element */
} GIF COLORTABLE;
```

- *Local image descriptor*: Each image has a local image descriptor before the image data. The structure of the local image descriptor is as follows:

```
typedef struct _GifImageDescriptor

{

BYTE Separator; /* Image Descriptor identifier */

WORD Left; /* X position of image on the display */

WORD Top; /* Y position of image on the display */

WORD Width; /* Width of the image in pixels */

WORD Height; /* Height of the image in pixels */

BYTE Packed; /* Image and Color Table Data Information */

} GIFIMGDESC;
```

The separator indicates the start of the image descriptor data block. The left and top are the coordinates of upper-left corner pixel of the image. These coordinates are considered (0, 0). The width and height indicates the image size in the pixels. The BYTE Packed Image and Color Table Data Information includes the following five subfields:

- Bit 0: local color table flag
- Bit 1: interlace flag
- Bit 2: sort flag
- Bit 3–4: reserved
- Bit 5–7: size of local color table entry
- *Local color table*: The local image descriptor is followed by the local color table. It has the same format as the global color table. Every element consists of the three colors: red, green, and blue.

    ```
    typedef struct _GifColorTable
    {
    BYTE Red; /* Red Color Element */
    BYTE Green; /* Green Color Element */
    BYTE Blue; /* Blue Color Element */
    } GIFCOLORTABLE;
    ```

- *Image data*: The image data in the GIF file is compressed by using the LZW compression algorithm. Data is encoded in a continuous stream, read from start to finish. It stores the data in a series of data subblocks. Each data block starts with the count byte. The count byte is between one and 255 and shows the number of data bytes in the subblock.

There are currently two versions of GIF:

- *GIF 87a*: The first version of GIF was generated in 1987. It uses the LZW file compression technique, and supports features such as interlacing, 256-color palettes, and multiple image storage.

- *GIF 89a*: This version was generated in 1989. It supports features like background transparency, delay times, and image replacement parameters. These features are useful for storing multiple images as animations.

JPEG (Joint Photographic Experts Group)

JPEG is a commonly used method to compress photographic images. It uses a compression algorithm to minimize the size of the file without affecting the quality of the image.

The JPEG file format is useful for the following applications: digital cinema, digital photography, printing and scanning, document imaging, medical imaging, wireless imaging, remote sensing and GIS, image archives and databases, facsimiles, surveillance, and prepress.

JPEG compression happens in four phases:

1. First, the JPEG algorithm divides the image in separate blocks of 8 × 8 pixels.

2. The compression algorithm then applies a discrete cosine transform (DCT) for the whole image. DCT exchanges the values of images for every pixel in each block to an 8 × 8 matrix of DCT coefficients.

3. Next, the compression algorithm checks the JPEG image quality asked for by the user, and then calculates two separate tables of quantization constants, one for luminance and one for chrominance. These constants quantize the DCT coefficients.

4. The last step is to compress these coefficients using a Huffman or arithmetic coding scheme.

JPEG File Structure

The first bits of a file identify the type of file. Every JPEG file starts with binary value 0xffd8 (SOI—start of image) and ends with binary value 0xffd9 (EOI—end of image), so ffd8 (the 0x is implied) shows that it is a JPEG file when viewed with a hex editor. A JPEG bitstream contains a sequence of data chunks, or segments, and every chunk starts with a marker value. The basic format of a segment is followed by the 16-bit integer value that determines the file size value. The most significant byte of the marker (the left-most bit) is 0xff. The lower byte of the marker determines the type of marker.

The basic format of a segment is as follows:

0xff + marker number (1 byte) + data size (2 bytes) + data (*n* bytes)

For example, for the marker FF E1 00 0E, the marker (0xFFE1) has 0x000E (which equals 14) bytes of data. But the data size 14 includes the data size descriptor (2 bytes); thus, only 12 bytes of data follow after 0x000E.

JPEG 2000

JPEG 2000 is a new version of JPEG compression from the JPEG committee. JPEG 2000 employs wavelet technology so images can be better compressed without affecting quality of an image. Finding JPEG 2000 formats on the Internet is uncommon, and thus is not often supported in popular Web browsers.

JPEG 2000 Features

- JPEG 2000 offers a 20 percent improvement in compression efficiency over the current JPEG format.

- It employs wavelet technology with the existing compression algorithm. Wavelet technology gives improved image quality and better compression.

- It offers lossless compression mode as an option. The size of the lossless JPEG 2000 image will be half the original image.

- This compression was developed mainly for use on the Internet.

- It can handle RGB, LAB, and CMYK formats with up to 256 channels of information.

BMP (Bitmap) File The BMP is a standard file format for a Windows DIB (Device Independent Bitmap) file. Microsoft developed this format to store bitmap files in DIB format so that on any kind of display, Windows can display it. Bitmap images can be animated. The size and color of these images can vary from 1 bit per pixel (black and white) to 24-bit color (16.7 million colors).

BMP File Structure Every bitmap file contains the following data structure:

- *File header*: The first part of the header that includes the data about the type, size, and layout of a file

- *Information header*: A header component that contains the dimensions, compression type, and color format for the bitmap

- *The RGBQUAD array*: A color table that comprises the array of elements equal to the colors present in the bitmap; this color table does not support bitmaps with 24 color bits, as each pixel is represented by 24-bit RGB values in the actual bitmap.

- *Image data*: The array of bytes that contains bitmap image data; image data comprises color and shading information for each pixel.

PNG (Portable Network Graphics) PNG is a lossless image format intended to replace the GIF and TIFF formats. PNG improves the GIF file format and replaces it with the image file format. It is copyright- and license-free.

PNG file format supports:

- 24-bit true color

- Transparency—both normal and alpha channel

PNG File Structure

- PNG File Signature:
  - PNG file signature shows that the remainder of a file has a single PNG image.
  - The images comprise a series of chunks, starting with an IHDR chunk and ending with an IEND chunk.

Chunk Layout

- Chunk layout follows the header.
- Each chunk in a set suggests some information about the image.

- Every chunk has a header specifying the size and type of chunk.
- Every chunk consists of four parts:
  - *Length*: a 4-byte unsigned integer that gives the number of bytes present in the chunk's data field
  - *Chunk type*: a 4-byte chunk type code
  - *Chunk data*: the data bytes appropriate to the chunk type, if any; this field can be of zero length.
  - *CRC (Cyclic Redundancy Check)*: a 4-byte CRC calculated on the preceding bytes in the chunk; it includes the chunk type code and chunk data fields, but not the length field.

TIFF (Tagged Image File Format) TIFF is a raster file format for digital images, created by Aldus, now controlled by Adobe. It was originally intended for use with PostScript printing. The main advantage of the TIFF file is that it can contain several image formats in a file. Tags are used to describe how the data should be represented in the final image.

The TIFF file can be used as a container for JPEG files. The file extension is .tif. TIFF supports both lossy and lossless compression algorithms; the lossless algorithms include PackBits and the LZW algorithm.

It has the following features:

- *Extendability*: This format can add new images and new information about the images without invalidating older image types.
- *Portability*: TIFF is flexible and platform-independent.
- *Revisability*: It was designed to efficiently exchange image information. It is also used as a native internal format for image editing applications.

TIFF File Structure TIFF files are composed of three data structures:

- *Image file header (IFH)*: The image file header is the first data structure in the TIFF.
  - This 8-byte image file header is fixed at the location offset zero. The first two bytes contain the information about byte ordering, which is very important when the file is created. It contains either two bytes of "II" (hex 4949) for an Intel-created image file, or "MM" (hex 4D4D), for a Motorola-created image file.
  - Versions in the IFH consist of the decimal value of 42_{10}. It verifies that the present file is TIFF or not. This number remains constant, but if someone changes it, it means the TIFF file format has been changed and TIFF reader becomes unable to read that file.
  - The last four bytes in the IFH give the number of bits from the start of the file to the image file directory structure.
  - Notice that nothing about the image itself is included in the IFH. All image information is stored in the image file directory.
- *Image file directory (IFD)*: The IFD holds all the information about an image. If the file contains more than one IFD, there is more than one image in the file.

- Each IFD entry consists of: a 16-bit header that tells the number of included tags, and all the directory entries (DEs) for a given image. Each DE is 12 bytes long.
- After all DEs have been listed, the remaining bytes include the offset to the next IFD. If it is the last IFD in the file, then the storage location of the offset is four bytes of zeros.

- *Directory entry (DE):* The DE is contained in the IFD. The DE is 12 bytes divided into four parts.
  - The first part is the tag field; it defines the raster data present in the TIFF files.
  - The next field is the type field, which specifies the data type of the image parameter, each having the integer number.
  - Length is the third field; it specifies the number of items of particular data types used. This value represents the number of data units in this particular entry; it does not represent the number of bytes needed to store the entry.
  - The last part of a DE contains the offset of the file to actual data related to the tag.

ZIP (Zone Information Protocol) ZIP is a method of compressing files designed by Phil Katz. Tools such as WinZip and WinRAR use this protocol to compress files. In ZIP, several files may be gathered together and compressed into a single "archive" file. A zipped file must be uncompressed in order to be used. Zip files can contain any file, such as text files, pictures, executables, and music, and can be password protected for security purposes.

Zip files contain all the information about a zipped file, such as the name of the file, its path, on which data it is created, related time, and last modification.

There are several advantages to Zip files:

- It compresses a number of files into a single file, which reduces the space on the hard disk.
- Zip files can be transmitted faster over a network.
- Several files can be transferred at once.

Data Compression in Image Files

Image file formats, like bitmaps, cannot compress data without the help of some compression tools. Some of the most popular image file formats use the Graphics Interchange Format (GIF) and Joint Photographic Experts Group (JPEG) to compress data. This saves disk space and reduces the time it would take to transfer the image from one system to another. Compression tools make the data compact and reduce the file size so drive space can be saved.

Data compression is a procedure that makes use of multifaceted algorithms used to reduce the file size. Typically, coding the data from a larger image to another smaller one is known as data compression. Vector quantization is similar to data compression. A vector image makes use of a mathematical equation that is similar to rounding up decimal values to eliminate unnecessary data.

Data compression is of interest in computer forensics because of its advantages in data processing, such as the cost savings and large volume of data manipulated in many business applications. The genre of local redundancy present in business data files comprise runs of zeros in numeric fields, series of blanks in alphanumeric fields, and fields present in some records and null in others.

Understanding File Compression

Most files use the same information, meaning they repeat the same sentences or words many times. File compression programs simply get rid of the redundancy. The file compression techniques list the information that is repeated, assign a code or number to each unique bit of information, and use the code to compress the information.

In this technique, repeated words are selected and stored into the dictionary. This dictionary consists of the words and numbers assigned to them. So when any word is repeated, the number is written, rather than the word. It is necessary to maintain the dictionary because the dictionary is used to decompress the file. Most compression methods use the LZW adaptive dictionary-based algorithm.

For example: The cat is in the tree.

    1   2   3   4   1   5

In the above example "the" word is repeated twice, so rather than write "the" two times, it is easier to give the number.

There are two main techniques of data compression:

- *Lossless compression*: **Lossless compression** maintains data integrity.
- *Lossy compression*: Lossy compression does not maintain data integrity.

Lossless Compression Algorithms

Huffman Coding Algorithm The **Huffman coding algorithm** is a fixed-to-variable length code algorithm. It takes input characters that have a fixed length and gives the output, which has a variable length. The main concept behind the algorithm is that short code words are assigned to those input blocks that have high probabilities, and long code words to those with low probabilities. The characters can be arranged in any way.

This algorithm combines two possible characters into a single possibility by adding the code word. This procedure is continued until only one character remains. The tree is formed, and from that code tree, the Huffman code is obtained. Huffman codes are not unique. You can assign any label, such as a label to the upper branches of zero, and to the lower branches a label of one.

This algorithm uses two possible characters. In the example below, these characters are zero and one. The values with the highest probability, a and e, have the shortest codes (00 and 10). The values with the lowest probability, j and b, have the longest codes (111111 and 111110). Once these values are compressed, the file will be shorter because there will be fewer long-code values in the resulting file than short-code values.

Figure 5-1 shows a possible Huffman coding system.

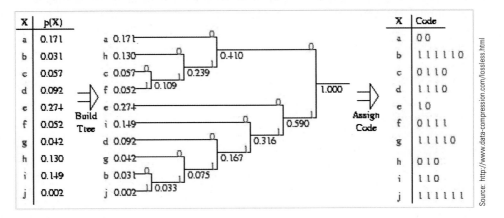

Figure 5-1 In this image, read the binary numbers backward to reach the letters, discounting the 1.000. For example, F is 0111.

LZW (Lempel-Ziv-Welch) Coding Algorithm

The LZW is used in most of the lossless compression techniques. LZW is a fixed-to-variable length code algorithm. Input is given in the variable length, while the output is given in the fixed length. It was generated not for a particular source, but for a large class of sources. In this algorithm, the input is given to the nonoverlapping blocks that have different lengths.

The following explains how to apply the encoding algorithm:

1. First, create a dictionary that contains all the blocks of one length, but all are nonoverlapping blocks (D={a,b}).
2. Find the longest block W present in the dictionary.
3. Encode that W, by its value present in the dictionary.
4. Add W, followed by the first symbol of the next block to the dictionary.
5. Return to step 2 and repeat the same procedure.

In this way, the final amount of bits needed to contain the same information is reduced.

Consider the following example.

A	000	E	100
B	001	F	101
C	011	G	110
D	111	STOP char	010

In this example, the word BEAD would be encoded 001/100/000/111/010. Remember that when you apply LZW, you bundle single length entries and add new codes. For some of these codes, you may need to expand the returned code length (e.g., adding another digit: 000 to 0000). Applying the LZW, the dictionary may be expanded to include the following entries:

AB	0000	AD	0101
BC	0001	AE	1010
CD	0011	AF	1001
DE	0111	AG	1011
EF	1111	BD	0110
FG	1110	BE	1101
AC	0100	STOP char	0010

Now the word BEAD would be encoded 1101/0101/0010, which is three bits shorter. If the dictionary is further expanded, the returned strings would get longer, but they include more values per string, and the overall length of the file is compressed.

Lossy Compression

Lossy compression is different from lossless compression, as it can compress data permanently by overlooking some parts of the data. However, data integrity is not maintained in the lossy data compression technique.

The lossy data compression technique is never used for text compression. When a JPEG file is saved under a different image format, lossy compression is used to compress the data. However, once the image file is decompressed, the user will lose a lot of information. Another form of lossy compression is when vectors are used to compress the file, known as **vector quantization**.

Vector Quantization Vector quantization is a lossy data compression technique. Vector quantization uses an algorithm to find out if the data can be disregarded based on vectors that are present in the image file. The algorithms used are based on the principle of block coding. In each block, the information is replaced by the approximate average value.

Figure 5-2 shows a sample of vector quantization. In this example, any value within a block that falls between −4 and −2 will return the value −3 (code 00). Therefore, any slight nuances to the image will be lost.

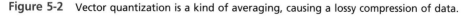

Figure 5-2 Vector quantization is a kind of averaging, causing a lossy compression of data.

Locating and Recovering Image Files

The first and most valid step that the forensic examiner must take is to search and recover any image files that are appropriate to the case at hand. Images are not necessarily present in standard image formats; therefore, investigators must also examine files that are of non-standard formats.

The Windows and DOS operating systems have a wide variety of tools that can recover image files. These tools search for and retrieve specific information that is embedded in the image itself. Every image file has a header, which gives programs instructions about how the image file should be displayed on the screen. When an image file is dispersed into many areas on the disk, the forensic investigator should recover all the fragments in order to regenerate the image file. Looking for pieces of a file is known as **salvaging**, and in some parts of North America it is called **carving**.

In order to carve image file data from free space in the disk, it is essential to know about data patterns. These enable a forensic investigator to identify image file fragments. In any forensic investigation, this would be the first step in locating image files. After recovering the parts of a fragmented image file, the next step is to restore the data fragments. The most common tool used for this purpose is DriveSpy. This tool is used to carve known data sets from the leftover recovered data. This information must be restored to view the image file.

Using DriveSpy to Locate and Recover Image File Fragments Computer forensic investigators use DriveSpy to locate and recover image file fragments. Investigators use the following simple steps to locate JPEG files on a disk:

1. Open a DOS command prompt window. Type in **DriveSpy** and press Enter to run the DriveSpy application.

2. At the DriveSpy SYS prompt, enter **Output Hdr_find.log** to enable the application to record the output of the commands that can be used in a text file named Hdr_find.log.

3. Insert the target investigation floppy disk into the A:\ drive. At the SYS prompt, type **Drive A**, and then press the Enter key to navigate to drive A:\.

4. From the DA command prompt, type **Part 1** and then press Enter to display the partition information for the floppy disk.

5. From the DAP1 command prompt, type **Search** *[filename]* (enter the file or folder name to look for) and press Enter. This will start a keyword search. At the prompt, press Y to turn off page mode.

From this process, the DriveSpy application searches the floppy disk for data that will match the search criteria, and can record this data in Hdr_find.log file. The log file can be viewed from Notepad.

Analyzing Image File Headers Investigators must analyze image file headers when normal forensic tools cannot recognize new file extensions. Hexadecimal values present in the header can be used to define a file type in DriveSpy. A hexadecimal editor, such as Hex Workshop, can help access the file header.

For instance, when an investigator encounters a .h9 Freehand file, the file headers section of DriveSpy.ini is not able to define the .h9 format. In order to determine the file type, the investigator will need to know the file's good header value. This can be found by comparing the existing file headers with file headers of another image file format. The investigator can then identify a tool that can rescue and display the image.

Repairing Damaged File Headers Investigators recover damaged remnants from free space on the drive. This information would be similar to headers from common image files. Header data that is partly overwritten can be used to repair damaged headers. The HEX Workshop application can be used to repair damaged headers.

Each image file has a special file header value that depends upon the format of the file type. An investigator can identify residual data from partially overwritten headers in file free space by examining common image header values. For example, the JPEG image file format has a hexadecimal value of FF D8 FF E0 00 10. Most JPEG files have the letters JFIF after the hexadecimal values of the file, as in FF D8 FF E0 00 10 JFIF. If a file fragment is found with JFIF, or the hexadecimal value associated with JPEG files, it is possible to identify the JPEG image.

Carving Data from Unallocated Space
Once a forensic investigator has identified data, a computer forensic program can carve, or retrieve, the fragmented image file. DriveSpy is the most popular tool used by forensic investigators for this purpose.

First, the investigator creates a duplicate bitstream copy of the original evidence files using Digital Intelligence Image. Once the target disk contains the complete image of the file, DriveSpy can locate the file on the original disk and carve the data from the unallocated space. The SaveSect command is then used to save the file as an external file.

Reconstructing File Fragments
Corruption of data prevents investigators from reconstructing file fragments from an image file. Data can be corrupted accidentally without the knowledge of the user of the computer, or the data can be corrupted intentionally. It is up to the forensic investigator to find out how the data was corrupted. File fragments can be reconstructed by using DriveSpy to examine a suspect disk. Investigators can then build the case based on the reconstructed data.

Many forensic investigations lead to the conclusion that the suspect has intentionally corrupted data in order to hide incriminating evidence. The suspect may have done this by corrupting cluster links in a FAT of a disk. A disk-editing tool can help a forensic investigator access the FAT and identify the corrupted cluster. Corrupted clusters display 0000 in the disk editor. Take the example of the screenshot shown in Figure 5-3 where the image file header is a bitmap (shown in the highlighted portion of the hexadecimal values).

Figure 5-3 shows the output of Hex Workshop when repairing a fragmented image file.

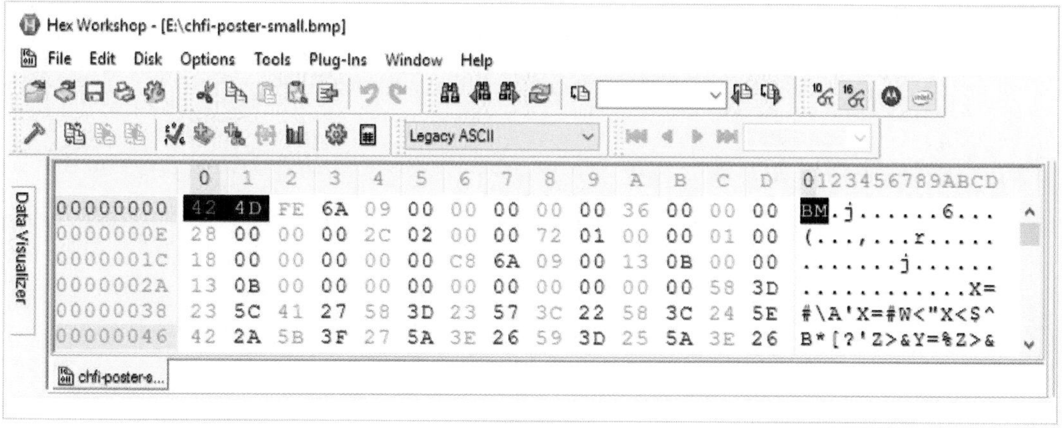

Figure 5-3 Fragmented data is encoded in hexadecimal. It can be repaired using a disk-editing tool.

Identifying Unknown File Formats Computer forensic investigators often come across unknown image file formats. The following is a list of nonstandard image file formats:

- Targa (.tga)
- Raster Transfer Language (.rtl)
- Photoshop (.psd)
- Illustrator (.ai)
- Freehand (.h9)
- Scalable vector graphics (.svg)
- Paintbrush (.pcx)

In order to find and view nonstandard image file formats, forensic investigators can use any search engine, using the image file extension, to identify and download a tool that can view the image.

The following tools can identify nonstandard file formats:

- FILExt
- IrfanView
- ACDSee
- ThumbsPlus
- AD Picture Viewer
- Picture Viewer Max
- FastStone Image Viewer
- XnView
- FACES—Sketch Software

Tool: FILExt FILExt is a quick way to identify the file type or parent application of a file based on the extension. On the FILExt Web site, enter the extension (for example, .lmp), and the application will return the most likely file type as well as some notes about the parent application and/ or history of the file type. Some even return header strings in hexadecimal. Some extensions, such as .crc, will return several possible parent applications or file types. A forensic investigator can use the header strings to confirm which of the returned file types it is.

Tool: Picture Viewer—IrfanView IrfanView is an image-viewing program that supports many nonstandard file formats including:

- Targa (.tga)
- Illustrator (.ai)
- Scalable vector graphics (.svg)
- FlashPix (.fpx)

Some notable features of IrfanView include:

- Ability to edit and add to images
- Various view options, including slideshow and thumbnail view

- Batch conversion
- Command line options
- Multipage TIFF editing and lossless JPEG rotation

Tool: ACDSee ACDSee is an image-viewing program that allows an investigator to find, view, manage, and edit images. With ACDSee version 9, investigators can also acquire image files, create PDFs, and view unknown file formats, including media files. ACDSee viewer displays images in full resolution.

Tool: ThumbsPlus ThumbsPlus is an image-cataloging program that enables an investigator to locate, view, edit, print, and organize images, metafiles, fonts, and movies.

Version 10 supports a variety of file formats, including:

- Common formats: TIFF, JPEG, PNG, RAW
- Photoshop (.psd), including documents loaded with plug-ins
- Various camera file formats
- Images loaded using new Cerious plug-ins
- Scanned images (TWAIN)

Tool: AD Picture Viewer AD Picture Viewer is a fast and compact image viewer for the Windows environment. It allows an investigator to view, print, organize, and manage images. It supports all popular graphic formats.

Tool: Picture Viewer Max Picture Viewer Max is an image and multimedia viewer for Windows 98/ME/2000/XP/Vista/7/8, and 10. It locates, views, edits, prints, organizes, sends and receives picture and image files, including videos, sounds, music, text files, documents, HTML, and system files. A forensic investigator can edit picture/image files using techniques such as flip, reverse, rotate, resize, brightness, contrast, color saturation, grayscale, hue, and other special effects and filters.

Some notable features of Picture Viewer Max are:

- It can add 3-D text and geometric shapes to pictures and images displayed in a multiple document interface.
- It can create blank picture frames with color gradients for logos or picture backgrounds.
- It supports: JPG, CMP, GIF, uncompressed TIF, TIFF, BMP, ICO, CUR, PCX, DCX, PCD, FPX, WMF, EMF, FAX, RAW, AWD, XPB, XPM, IFF, PBM, CUT, PSD, PNG, TGA, EPS, RAS, WPG, PCT, PCX, CLP, XWD, FLC, ANI, SGI, XBM, MAC, IMG, MSP, CAL, ICA, SCT, SFF, SMP, TXT, BAT, LST, WRI, SYS, RTF, HTM, HTML, PSP, ASP, DOC, PDF, AVI, AVI(DivX), MPG, MPEG, MOV, MP3, M3U, ASX, ASF, MID, RMI, MP2, AIFF, M1V, WMA, and WMV.
- It can convert picture file formats between picture file types.
- It can print up to eight pictures on a page, with titles for each page and picture. Select your font and color for all printed text.
- It can receive pictures and Zip files by e-mail, and view, edit, save, and print with Picture Viewer Max.

Tool: FastStone Image Viewer The FastStone Image Viewer is an image browser, converter, and editor. It has a nice array of features that include: image viewing, management, comparison, red-eye removal, e-mailing, resizing, cropping, and color adjustments.

Some notable features of FastStone Image Viewer are:

- Image modification tools: Resize/resample, rotate/flip, crop, sharpen/blur, brightness/contrast
- Support for all major graphic formats (BMP, JPEG, JPEG 2000, animated GIF, PNG, PCX, TIFF, WMF, ICO, and TGA), and popular digital camera RAW formats (CRW, CR2, NEF, PEF, RAF, MRW, ORF, SRF, and DNG)
- High-quality magnification and a musical slideshow with 150+ transitional effects
- Image annotation and scanner support
- Image color effects: grayscale, sepia, negative, RGB adjustment
- Image special effects: watermark, annotation, drop shadows, framing, bump map, lens, morph, waves
- Image management, including tagging capability, with drag-and-drop and copy to/move to folder support
- Versatile screen capture capability

Tool: XnView The XnView tool can display and convert graphics files. It supports more than 400 graphics formats. Versions of it support Windows, Mac OS X, Linux x86, Linux ppc, FreeBSD x86, OpenBSD x86, NetBSD x86, Solaris sparc, Solaris x86, Irix mips, HP-UX, and AIX.

XnView includes the following features:

- It can import about 400 graphics file formats and export about 50 graphics file formats.
- It can support multipage TIFF, animated GIF, and animated ICO, as well as Image IPTC and EXIF metadata.
- It can support resize, rotate, and crop.
- It includes support for auto levels and contrast.
- The user can apply filters and effects (e.g., blur, average, emboss, lens, wave) and modify the number of colors.
- It supports full-screen mode.
- It has support to create or edit multipage files (TIFF, DCX, LDF).
- It prints, drags and drops, and has 44 languages in Windows.

Tool: FACES—Sketch Software FACES contains a database of more than 3,850 facial features, including tools and accessories. This utility allows you to compose many images with their permutations and combinations. Law enforcement agencies use the software to identify suspects.

The features included in the software are coded in morphological order, and allow you to design images or faces of your choice with ease. One of the main features of this software is the utility InterCode, which encrypts the composite image and converts it into a character

ID code. There exists a unique InterCode with every original image. When you click in the InterCode, a corresponding composite image appears on the screen. Thus, the software performs the process in seconds. This software is primarily used by law enforcement agencies and crime branch investigation organizations in identifying suspects.

Steganography in Image Files

Since the introduction of the Internet, hidden messages inside digital images have become the most common and highly effective form of steganography. Images are stored as a group of pixels, 8–24 bits per pixel. This group of pixels can be stored in a second image file in one of three ways.

There are also three methods that are used to hide the messages inside these images:

1. Least-significant-bit method
2. Filtering and masking
3. Algorithms and transformation

Steganalysis

Steganalysis is the reverse process of steganography. Steganography hides the data, while steganalysis is used to detect the data hidden via steganography. Steganalysis determines the encoded hidden message and, if possible, recovers that message. The message can be detected by looking at variances between bit patterns and unusually large file sizes.

There are two main challenges of steganalysis:

- The data may have been encrypted before it was hidden.
- If some of the signal or file contains noise or irrelevant data encoded into it, steganalysis can be complicated and take longer.

Tool: Hex Workshop The Hex Workshop is a set of hexadecimal development tools for Microsoft Windows, combining advanced binary editing with the ease and flexibility of a word processor. With Hex Workshop, forensic investigators can edit, cut, copy, paste, insert, and delete hex; print customizable hex dumps; and export to RTF or HTML for publishing. Additionally, investigators can go to, find, replace, compare, and calculate checksums and character distributions within a sector or file.

Hex Workshop is integrated with Windows Explorer so investigators can hex-edit from the most frequently used workspaces. Hex Workshop includes a Base Converter for converting between hex, decimal, and binary, and a Hex Calculator supporting arithmetic and logical operations. The Hex Workshop also contains a Data Inspector and Structure Viewer so examiners can view and edit interpreted decimal values and embedded arithmetic and logical operations, allowing direct manipulation of the data.

Some features of the Hex Workshop application include:

1. A highly customizable editing environment
2. Data in its natural and native structured form as viewed through the Structure Viewer
3. Dynamic bookmarks in a simple macro language
4. The ability to edit sectors of floppies and hard disks

5. Prints high-quality hex dumps with customized headers, footers, and fonts

6. Views and edits raw binary data as decimal values with the Data Inspector

7. Interprets values in either little-endian (e.g., Intel) or big-endian (e.g., Motorola) byte ordering

8. Manipulates data using one of 22 embedded operations: byteflip, inverse bits, left shift, right shift, rotate left, rotate right, block shift left, block shift right, XOR, OR, AND, change sign, plus, minus, multiply, divide, mod, setfloorvalue, setceilingvalue, uppercase, lowercase, and swapcased

9. Inserts external file contents or save a block of data as a new file

10. Changes are tracked and coded in color

11. Exports and copies hex as RTF, text, and HTML for publishing or as C source or Java source

12. Imports and exports Intel hex code and Motorola S-Records.

13. Finds and replaces hex, bitmasks, decimal, or ASCII (including Unicode) values

14. Easily navigates documents and sectors using the goto command

15. Views text interpretations under ASCII, DOS, EBCDIC, Macintosh, Windows, and Unicode character set filters

16. A binary compare tool to find differences in files

17. Calculates checksums and digests (MD2, MD4, MD5, SHA1) for all or part of a file

18. Views character distributions and exports results as tabbed text or comma-separated values

19. File/disk properties with the click of the mouse

20. File/disk attributes in the status bar

21. Online help including multiple character tables and list of data types and ranges

Figure 5-4 shows the Hex Workshop application.

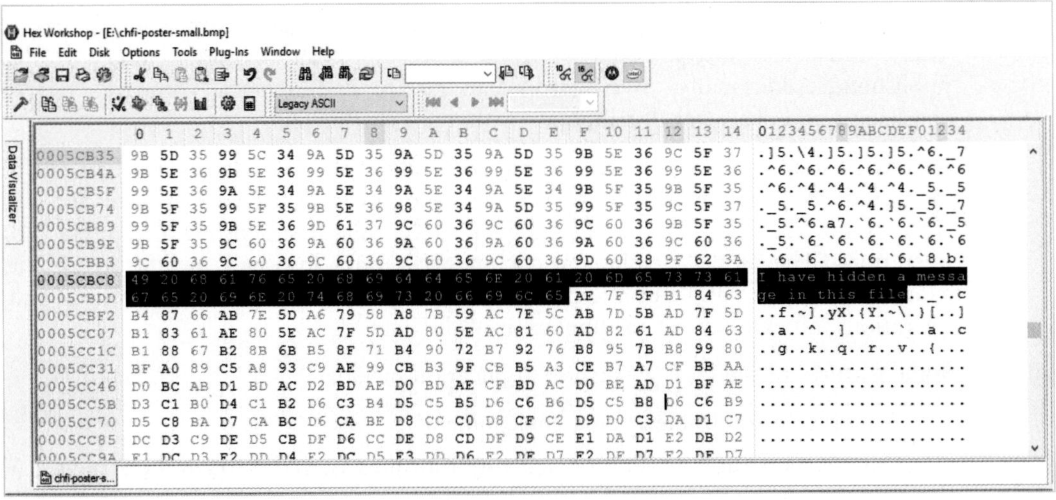

Figure 5-4   Hex Workshop is one of the most popular applications for steganalysis and image recovery.

Tool: Stegdetect

Stegdetect is used for the detection of steganographic content in an image. Stegdetect supports linear discriminant analysis. **Linear discriminant analysis** is the technique that determines the stego image that contains the hidden data. It detects different steganographic methods to embed hidden information in JPEG images.

Stegdetect supports several different feature vectors, and automatically computes receiver operating characteristics, which can be used to evaluate the quality of the automatically learned detection function.

Can penetrate information hidden using applications such as jsteg, jphide (UNIX and Windows), Invisible Secrets, Outguess v.01.3b, F5, appendX, and Camouflage.

Tool: ILook v8

ILook is a multithreaded, Unicode-compliant image file forensic investigation tool. It recovers images from seized computer systems or other digital media quickly. It is also used to detect images obtained from forensic imaging tools that produce a raw bitstream image. It supports Windows 2000 or Windows XP 32-bit platforms and the Windows Server 2003 64-bit platform.

Some features of ILook include:

- Identification and support of the following file systems: FAT12, FAT16, FAT32, FAT32x, VFAT, NTFS, HFS, HFS+, Ext2FS, Ext3FS, SysV AFS, SysV EAFS, SysV HTFS, CDFS, Netware NWFS, ReiserFS, and ISO9660
- An Internet Explorer–like interface allowing an investigator to view and navigate the file system as it originally appeared on the suspect's computer
- Granular extraction facilities that allow all or part of a file system to be extracted from an image
- Fast, sophisticated, regular expression search engine
- Built-in multiformat file viewing
- Password and pass-phrase dictionary generators
- File salvage (carve) capabilities
- Orphaned FAT directory recovery
- Hash analysis functions
- Data tagging and categorization features
- Case and evidence management features and multievidential item handling
- Internet cache and mailbox deconstruction functions
- Additional imager built into ILook for imaging directly attached devices
- File filtering and elimination functions
- Search-results database stores the results of all searches run against any item in a case

Tool: P2 eXplorer

Paraben's P2 eXplorer allows an investigator to mount a forensic image and explore it as though it were a drive. The image is not just mounted to view logical files, but is mounted as the actual bitstream image, preserving unallocated, slack, and deleted data.

P2 eXplorer is able to:

- Mount compressed and encrypted Paraben's Forensic Replicator (PFR) images, and several images at a time
- Mount PFR, EnCase images (up to v4.02), SafeBack 1 and 2 images, WinImage non-compressed images and RAW images from Linux dd and other tools
- Support dynamic drive images and both logical and physical image types
- Autodetect image format
- Shell support easy mounting/unmounting as well as mounting over a network
- Write-protect for preserving evidence
- MD5 checksum verify and hash verify

Identifying Copyright Issues with Graphics

Section 106 of the 1976 Copyright Act gives the owner of a graphic or image copyright the exclusive right to do and to authorize any of the following:

- Reproduce the copyrighted work in copies or phonorecords;
- Prepare derivative works based upon the copyrighted work;
- Distribute copies or phonorecords of the copyrighted work to the public by sale or other transfer of ownership, or by rental, lease, or lending;
- In the case of literary, musical, dramatic, and choreographic works, pantomimes, and motion pictures and other audiovisual works, perform the copyrighted work publicly;
- In the case of literary, musical, dramatic, and choreographic works, pantomimes, and pictorial, graphic, or sculptural works, including the individual images of a motion picture or other audiovisual work, display the copyrighted work publicly; and
- In the case of sound recordings, perform the work publicly by means of a digital audio transmission.

Chapter Summary

- An image is an artifact that reproduces the likeness of some subject.
- A file format is a particular way to encode information for storage in a computer file.
- Standard image file formats include JPEG, GIF, BMP, TIFF, and PNG.
- Data compression means encoding the data to take up less storage space and less bandwidth for transmission.
- Data compression is performed by using a complex algorithm to reduce the size of a file.
- Lossy compression compresses data permanently by removing information contained in the file.
- Image files have a unique file header value. Common image header values have residual data from partially overwritten headers in file slack.

Key Terms

bitmap (BMP)

carving

CMYK

dithering

Graphic Interchange Format (GIF)

grayscale

Huffman coding algorithm

indexed color

interlacing

Joint Photographic Experts Group (JPEG) file format

Lempel-Ziv-Welch (LZW) algorithm

limited color palette

linear discriminant analysis

lossless compression

lossy compression

pixel

Portable Network Graphics (PNG)

raster image

Red-Green-Blue (RGB) color model

salvaging

steganalysis

Tagged Image File Format (TIFF)

vector images

vector quantization

Zone Information Protocol (ZIP)

5

Review Questions

1. Describe three differences between vector images and raster images.

    _____

    _____

    _____

    _____

2. Name three image file formats and name whether each is vector, raster, or both.

    _____

    _____

    _____

    _____

3. How does file compression work?

    _____

    _____

    _____

    _____

4. What is the difference between lossless and lossy data compression? Which would you use with text files?

_____

_____

_____

_____

5. Describe two main differences between the LZW and Huffman coding systems.

_____

_____

_____

_____

6. When you analyze image file headers, what are you looking for?

_____

_____

_____

_____

7. What does carving mean?

_____

_____

_____

_____

8. Name a steganalysis tool and describe how it works.

_____

_____

_____

_____

9. How do you reconstruct file fragments?

_____

_____

_____

_____

10. List three different image file forensic tools. Describe why you would use each.

_____

_____

_____

_____

Hands-On Projects

1. Use the S-Tools program to hide a text file inside an image file:
   - Navigate to Chapter 5 in MindTap or on the Student Resource Center.
   - Download, unzip, and launch the S-Tools program.
   - Locate an image file saved in .bmp format and save it to your desktop.
   - Drag the .bmp image file into the S-Tools window.
   - Create a text file with a one-line message.
   - Drag the .txt file onto the image file in the S-Tools window.
   - Enter a passphrase and select an encryption algorithm and then click "**Ok.**"
   - Right-click in the hidden data window and save the image now containing a hidden message.
   - Compare the before and after image files for differences such as visual differences, differences in file size, etc.
   - Prepare a one-paragraph summary detailing your steganography efforts using S-Tools.

2. Use the S-Tools program to reveal a text file hidden inside an image file:
   - Launch the S-Tools program.
   - Drag a .bmp image containing a hidden message into the S-Tools window.
   - Right-click on the image and select "**Reveal.**"
   - Enter the passphrase and the encryption algorithm and then click "**Ok.**"
   - If the passphrase and encryption algorithm match, the hidden .txt file will be revealed.
   - Right-click and save the .txt file containing the hidden message.
   - Prepare a one-paragraph summary analyzing the usefulness of this tool to create and reveal hidden messages.

3. Use Hex Workshop to identify the format of a graphic file:
   - Using your preferred Internet browser, navigate to _http://www.bpsoft.com/downloads/_ and download and install the latest version of Hex Workshop.
   - Start Hex Workshop and select "**File,**" "**Open.**"
   - Navigate to a graphic file you have located and saved ahead of time.
   - Select the graphic file and click "**Open.**"

The first logical sector will contain identifying information to indicate the graphic file format. In the example below, "BM" is displayed in the first logical sector, indicating that this is a .bmp file (Figure 5-5).

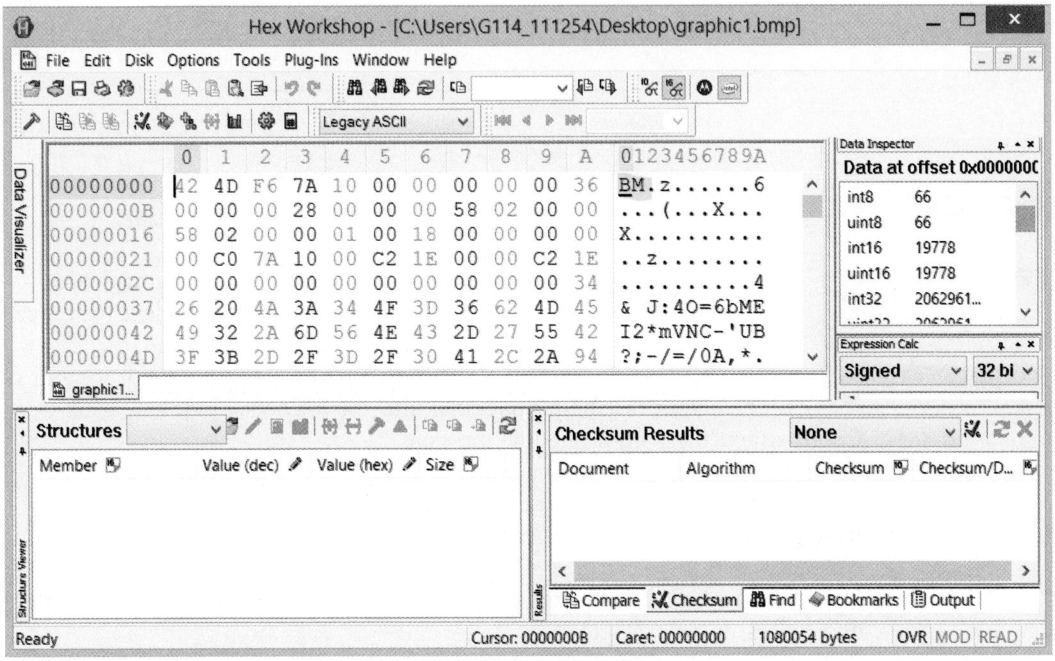

Source: Hex Workshop

Figure 5-5 Hex Workshop output identifying format of graphic file.

- Analyze three additional graphic files of different formats in Hex Workshop to identify the graphic file type.
- Prepare a one-paragraph summary detailing the results of your efforts.

Glossary

bitmap (BMP) a raster-based image format closely associated with Microsoft and many Microsoft image programs save files as BMPs by default. BMP files typically do not compress well, and so are larger than other compressed formats.

carving *see* salvaging

checksum (also called a hash sum) a fixed-size integer resulting from the application of an algorithm to a block of digital data for the purpose of verifying the integrity of the original data; often used when comparing copied data with the original data

CMYK a color model that stands for Cyan, Magenta, Yellow, and Key (black); also known as the four-color model, CMYK works by subtracting some colors from white (all colors), leaving the resulting hue. CMYK is a model used by commercial printers and is capable of rendering millions of colors.

cover medium the medium used to hide a message with steganography

cyclic redundancy check (CRC) a type of function that takes a quantity of data of any size and produces an output of a fixed length, usually a 32-bit integer that is generally used to verify the integrity of the original data

data acquisition the act of taking possession of or obtaining control of data and adding it to a collection of evidence

data duplication the act of making a copy of data already acquired to preserve the original evidence in pristine condition

digital watermark a digital stamp embedded into a digital signal

dithering a method used to create the illusion of greater color depth by blending a smaller number of colored dots together

Graphic Interchange Format (GIF) an 8-bit RGB bitmap format for images with up to 256 distinct colors per frame

grayscale images in grayscale only include intensity information. Only shades of black and white (or gray) are rendered.

hashing a well-defined mathematical function that converts a large variable-sized amount of data into a small fixed-length integer that may serve as an index into an array, as a method of obscuring and protecting passwords being transferred over a network, or to verify the integrity of stored data; Message Digest v5 (MD5) and Secure Hashing Algorithm (SHA) are two of the most common hashing functions

Huffman coding algorithm a variable-to-fixed lossless compression algorithm

indexed color a color system in which every color is coded to a specific number (or index)

interlacing a mechanism that makes images appear faster on-screen by first displaying a low-resolution version of the image and gradually showing the full version

Joint Photographic Experts Group (JPEG) file format a raster image compression format

least significant bit (LSB) a steganography technique in which the rightmost bit in the binary notation is substituted with a bit from the embedded message

Lempel-Ziv-Welch (LZW) algorithm a variable-to-fixed compression algorithm used in GIF files

limited color palette each color in the GIF color table is described in RGB values, with each value having a range between zero and 255

linear discriminant analysis a method of classification by comparing two or more samples; in Stegdetect software, it identifies the steganography by comparing the two images

lossless compression describes a compression algorithm that maintains data integrity

lossy compression describes a compression algorithm that does not maintain data integrity, leading to possible loss of data

pixel short for *picture element*, a pixel is a single point in a graphic image. On monitors, pixels are arranged in rows and columns to display pictures and text. To display a picture, pixels on the screen are closely connected.

Portable Network Graphics (PNG) a lossless, well-compressed format for displaying raster graphics; PNGs were created to replace GIFs. They support alpha channels and generally have smaller file sizes than the older GIF format.

raster image a file in which the information is converted into pixels; raster images are nonscalable

Recycle Bin a space on a disk for files and folders that are marked for deletion

recycled folder a folder on each drive to which files deleted by compliant programs are moved

Red-Green-Blue (RGB) color model the representation of colors based on combinations of red, green, and blue; this model is generally used in monitors, cameras, and televisions and is less likely in print production

salvaging reconstructing an image file that was accidentally or deliberately destroyed using file fragments; synonymous with *carving*

security identifier (SID) a unique name assigned by a Windows domain controller to identify a specific computer on a network

sparse data copy a copy that an investigator makes of only part of a large set of data in which only the data pertinent to the investigation is included, in order to reduce the overall size of the evidence file; this technique is often used when copying data from RAID arrays, when dealing with terabytes or petabytes of information, or when only specific evidence is needed

steganalysis retrieving information hidden in image files

steganography the practice of embedding hidden messages within a carrier medium

stego-key the secret key used to encrypt and decrypt messages hidden by steganography

stego-medium the combined cover medium and embedded message used in steganography

stegosystem the mechanism used in performing steganography packet

Tagged Image File Format (TIFF) a flexible raster image file format, commonly used in desktop publishing and photography, that allows for multiple modes of compression and color depths

Transmission Control Protocol (TCP) a protocol that implements a core set of rules that allow reliable connection-oriented connections between host computers over a network

undelete to restore the content in files that have been deleted deliberately or accidentally from a disk

User Datagram Protocol (UDP) a nonreliable protocol that implements a best-effort set of rules that allow for network communication where exact delivery of each packet is not critical, such as for streaming video

vector images images in which information is stored as mathematical expressions rather than pixels; because the calculations can be done for any given space, vector images are scalable

vector quantization a lossy data compression technique in which vectors are used to compress the file

Zone Information Protocol (ZIP) a method of compressing computer data or files to save space

Index